The Modern Leader's Journey

The Modern Leader's Journey

A Coach's Guide to Presence and Impact in Turbulent Times

By Kathryn Lowell

The Modern Leader's Journey:
A Coach's Guide to Presence and Impact in Turbulent Times

Published by Kathryn Lowell Leadership Press

ISBN: 979-8-9930696-0-9 (paperback)
ISBN: 979-8-9930696-3-0 (hardcover)
ISBN: 979-8-9930696-1-6 (ebook)

For information, contact:
Kathryn Lowell Leadership Press
Bentonville, Arkansas
www.modernleadersjourney.com

Cover design and interior design by Alan Hebel

Printed in the United States of America

*For my clients, past, present, and those still to come.
Your willingness to grow, to face fear, and to lead
with integrity has been my greatest teacher.*

TABLE OF CONTENTS

PREFACE

My Journey From Image to Substance

Since 2001, I've had the extraordinary privilege of serving clients as both an image consultant and an executive coach. This dual perspective has shaped my entire approach, helping leaders align both how they show up on the surface and how they operate from within.

Early in my client work, I helped clients refine their outer appearance: how they entered a room, communicated credibility, and made first impressions count. But over time, I discovered something deeper.

Presence isn't just about polish. It's primarily about integrity—the alignment between who you are and how you lead.

That realization shifted my work from surface to substance, from checking boxes to asking deeper questions:

- Who am I when I lead?
- What energy do I bring into the room?
- What legacy am I leaving, not just in outcomes but in how people feel around me?

Having this dual lens has allowed me to witness and support deeply transformative journeys that have helped individuals align their external presence with their internal values. What began as a passion for helping people step into their power has evolved into the most meaningful professional journey I could have imagined.

Over the years, I've worked with professionals across industries, roles, and stages of growth. Many of these clients have become cherished friends. Our coaching conversations have reshaped how I define leadership—not as performance but as presence. And not just in metrics but in the emotional imprint we leave behind.

These are people who care deeply about doing good work, leading well, and growing with integrity. And if I've learned anything from them, it's this:

- Even the most accomplished leaders sometimes doubt themselves.

- Even the smartest voices go quiet in the room.

- Even those at the top can feel invisible, uncertain, or stuck.

That gap—between outer success and inner confidence—is what this book addresses. Closing that gap often requires a reset: trading fear and self-doubt for clarity and presence in a world unsettled by AI and galloping change.

The stories and tools I've included here reflect what I witness in real coaching settings every day. You'll find strategies, yes, but also research-based ideas, reflection prompts, and practical tools and habits for becoming a more grounded, visible, and trustworthy version of yourself.

I've also drawn from my own spiritual path—a journey that began in Christianity and has since expanded to include the wisdom and illumination of teachers like Ram Dass, the channeled wisdom of Seth, Abraham, the Guides of Paul Selig, and core principles from Buddhist, Hindu, and Taoist traditions. I believe that true leadership transcends metrics and titles; it's about presence, intention, and the legacy we leave in the hearts of others. This belief inspired the inclusion of "spiritual cues" throughout the book—brief moments of deeper reflection, designed to help you reconnect with what matters most.

The stories in this book are drawn from actual professional experiences. To protect privacy and maintain confidentiality, names, roles, industries, and details have been camouflaged. In some cases, client stories are composites—carefully crafted to reflect patterns I've seen repeatedly across many coaching journeys. Every effort has been made to preserve the emotional truth and complexity of the work my clients do—and the courage it takes to grow.

Whether you're beginning your career or navigating the long view, my hope is that this book serves as a companion on your journey toward purposeful leadership.

ACKNOWLEDGMENTS

This book exists thanks to the leaders who trusted me with their growth and allowed their journeys to shape these pages. To every client who has invited me into the real work of change: Thank you for your courage, candor, and persistence. Many of the stories here are composites or they are anonymized to protect privacy, but the truths remain intact.

Special thanks to the clients who offered direct feedback that sharpened specific chapters and ideas: Judd Semingson, Everline Ouma, Jason Fremstad, and Venessa Yates. Your insights on scalability, communication, culture, and the weight of leadership at higher levels strengthened this manuscript and the tools within it.

I'm also indebted to my reviewers, whose thoughtful reads and generous suggestions made this a better book. I offer my appreciation to Will Motazedi for his cross-generational lens and detailed commentary, and to Robert Burns, Cindy Moehring, Michael Spivey, and Olivia Spivey for their valuable notes and field-tested perspectives. And to Isabella Spivey and Amy Thrasher for their sharp eyes in editing.

Finally, the heartbeat of this book is forged in every reader doing the work—especially those who were promoted before they felt ready or who succeeded publicly while wrestling privately—and in your willingness to practice, to ask for feedback, and to keep going. May it meet you where you are and move you forward.

INTRODUCTION

Building Leadership Presence
From the Inside Out

You'd never guess it, but I used to be afraid to talk on the phone. I would blush so hard when called on in school that I'd completely lose my train of thought.

I was a smart kid—the kind who got straight A's, followed the rules, and read everything. But I lacked early social experience. No preschool. No playdates. I was an only child, raised by older parents, and spent most of my early years in quiet spaces— outside alone or with adults who loved me but didn't teach me how to be with peers.

So when I entered school, I already knew my letters and numbers, but I was socially unprepared. I didn't know how to interact with my peers and teachers. I felt watched. Exposed. Self-conscious. My body betrayed me constantly with flushed skin, a shaky voice, and runaway thoughts. I learned to hide it, for the most part. Eventually, I learned to adapt. I even made friends.

But inside? Fear. Constant, low-grade fear. Fear of being asked to speak and not knowing what to say. Fear of being too much or not enough.

That deep fear stayed with me. Even as I graduated from Yale. Even as I worked on Wall Street. Even as I sat across the table from powerful clients in powerful rooms wearing all the right clothes, doing all the right things.

I didn't know it then, but I was learning something I now see all the time in my clients. You can look accomplished and still feel unsure. You can appear confident and still be fearful. You can be moving up the corporate ladder and still feel like you're faking it. That gap between how we're perceived and how we feel is what this book is about.

The Outer Success–Inner Fear Gap

Now, decades later, I work with incredibly accomplished professionals who are facing the same things I did. They've checked every box. They've climbed fast. But still, they walk into high-stakes rooms and feel like they're performing. Even now, they flinch when they must give a presentation. They worry they're not "executive" enough—not ready, strong, smooth, or wherever else they may lack confidence.

These aren't problems of intelligence, effort, or competence.

These are problems of presence. The reality is, most people were never taught how real leadership presence looks and feels, or how to build it without faking it.

Planting the Seeds of Confidence

During business school at UCLA, I had a moment that changed everything. I was presenting in front of the class—something financial that was in my comfort zone—and afterward, the professor pulled me aside.

"You were really good," he said. "Convincing. Engaging. You should do more of that."

That one remark planted the first real seed of confidence in me. Not the kind you arm yourself with. Not the kind you bluff your way into. But the kind that comes from being seen and finally starting to believe in yourself.

That's what I want for you.

How This Book is Different

Before coaching leaders, I spent years in corporate finance, then pivoted into image consulting, where I helped professionals refine their presence through appearance, body language, and nonverbal cues. I still believe those things matter. But I discovered early on that the most important signal in any room isn't what you're wearing. It's your energy.

The leaders who truly command trust don't just look the part. They move with clarity. They speak with intention. They transmit presence before they ever say a word.

That's what this book is about.

It's not another executive presence book that reduces leadership to checklists about performance and polish. It's a guide to building a version of leadership that fits you—one that holds up under pressure, connects with others, and frees you to lead without overcompensating or playing small.

What to Expect

This book begins with fear because that's where most leadership distortion starts. But the book ends with something far more powerful than fear: grounded, visible, sustainable presence. Along the way, we'll explore:

- **Fear.** How it shapes behavior, even in high performers, and quietly erodes presence

- **Blind spots.** How to shift how others experience you, without losing yourself

- **Confidence.** What it really looks like, and how to stop chasing it
- **Perception.** Why being competent isn't enough if you're not being seen
- **Gravitas and energy.** How to lead without overworking or overexplaining
- **Peer dynamics.** The overlooked arena of influence that most leaders ignore
- **Coaching as culture.** How to lead others without controlling them
- **Legacy and identity.** How to rise without losing yourself along the way

You'll find:

- **Research-based insights**
- **Coaching stories** from real client journeys
- **Actionable models and frameworks** like the **Fear-to-Presence Model**, the **Hidden Job Description**, and the **Gravitas Spectrum**
- **Reader-to-Leader** prompts to help you apply what you're learning
- **And brief spiritual cues** to invite reflection, alignment, and deeper presence

At its core, this is a leadership book. But it's also a mirror. A strategy guide. A truth-teller. A permission slip. It's written for anyone who's ready to lead with more presence.

This book is for you if you've ever looked around a room and thought, "I'm not sure I belong here." If you've been told you are smart but "not quite leadership material." If you're tired of performing confidence and ready to embody it instead.

This book is here to help you close the gap between the leader you are and the one you're ready to become.

Let's begin.

MODELS AND FRAMEWORKS

This book includes a set of signature models and practical frameworks, collected here for quick reference. In addition, each chapter features recurring elements designed to guide practice, including **Reader-to-Leader**™ prompts (reflection and action steps), Field Notes, Coaching Cues, and Spiritual Cues. These are not listed chapter by chapter here, but they appear consistently throughout the book as part of the learning design.

All models and frameworks not otherwise attributed are Kathryn Lowell's intellectual property. Trademarked entries are marked here with ™.

SIGNATURE MODELS

Chapter 1: Fear-to-Presence Model™
Five stages from reactivity to grounded leadership presence

Chapter 2: Johari Window (Joseph Luft and Harrington Ingham)
The quadrants of awareness: open, hidden, blind, unknown

Chapter 3: Three Circles of Energy (Patsy Rodenburg)
A model contrasting withdrawn, broadcast, and present energy states

Chapter 4: Hidden Job Description™
The unwritten expectations that shape promotion paths

Chapter 6: Four Dimensions of Energy (adapted from Tony Schwartz)
Physical, emotional, mental, spiritual energy domains

Chapter 7: AI Disruption Equation™
When tech acceleration and identity ambiguity collide with presence

Chapter 8: Gravitas Spectrum™
A continuum of gravitas: underpowered, balanced, overbearing

Chapter 9: Listening Levels Model
From passive hearing to transformative listening

Chapter 10: Visibility Loop
The cycle of presence and relational resonance

Chapter 11: Five Coaching Shifts for Executives
Moves from directive to multiplier leadership

Chapter 12: Mind Flip
A shift from solving problems to navigating polarities

Chapter 12: Courage Container™
Holding tension between challenge and ease

Chapter 13: Executive Embodiment Model
Embodiment dimensions that signal leadership presence

Chapter 14: Three Frequencies of Culture
Control, connection, clarity as cultural tones

Chapter 15: Bridges Transitions Model (William Bridges)
The three stages of transition: ending, neutral zone, new beginning

Chapter 17: Integration Model
Awareness → Embodiment → Amplification → Transmission

PRACTICAL FRAMEWORKS AND TOOLS

Chapter 5: Leading Across a Matrix
Navigating peer politics and lateral influence

Chapter 5: Peer Influence Web
A framework for seeing how peer dynamics shape impact

Chapter 6: Micro Resets
Quick energy and emotional recalibration tools

Chapter 7: Leading Through Tech Disruption
Preserving trust and human leadership as technology reshapes work

Chapter 7: Future-Proofing Your Leadership
Human capabilities that remain essential as AI reshapes work

Chapter 8: The Presence Landscape
Distinguishes between presence, gravitas, charisma, and executive presence

Chapter 8: Gravitas Builders
Five ways to strengthen gravitas under pressure

Chapter 8: Three-Part Meeting Presence
Rituals for meetings: before, during, after

Chapter 9: Response Toolkit / Three-Part Recovery / Daily Warm-Ups
Communication tools and recovery strategies for presence under pressure

Chapter 9: The Four-Second Reset
A rapid tool to pause, regulate, and respond

Chapter 10: Real-Time Speaking Presence
Regulating your body and voice under live pressure

Chapter 11: Everyday Coaching Habits
Daily practices that embed a coaching culture

Chapter 12: Three-Minute Polarity Check
A quick reflection tool to reframe tension

Chapter 13: Rehearsal for the Room
A thirty-second ritual to center before key moments

Chapter 15: Sphere of Control (adapted from Stoic philosophy)
A framework for focusing energy on what leaders can influence

Chapter 15: Disruption GROW (adapted from Sir John Whitmore)
Applying the GROW sequence to lead through disruption

Chapter 15: Retirement Glide Path
Designing transitions with presence and purpose

Chapter 17: Monthly Leadership Mirror™
A practice for monthly leadership reflection and alignment

FEAR IN THE CLIMB

The Silent Companion to Ambition

Fear doesn't always show up the way we expect it to. It doesn't always come with shaky hands or a quiver in the voice. In high-achieving professionals, it's often quieter and skillfully hidden.

Sometimes, fear looks like rereading an email six times before hitting send. Tension in your jaw before a meeting. Smiling while your stomach tightens. Holding your opinion until you're sure it's perfect. Working late so no one can question your commitment.

I've spent years coaching senior leaders across industries—thoughtful, driven people operating in complex environments loaded with high expectations. And I've come to recognize what fear looks like in those places: not panic or paralysis but overpreparing. Overworking. Avoiding conflict. Shrinking in meetings. Waiting for certainty. Taking on too much so no one questions your value. It's not always dramatic. It's often subtle, polished, and running the show quietly in the background.

Unchecked and unexamined, fear becomes a quiet architect of leadership behavior. It shapes how we show up, communicate, and lead. Most dangerously, it limits the full expression of presence—that steady, felt quality that builds trust and draws others in.

This chapter is about recognizing how fear operates in your leadership—not just in big moments, but in the subtle patterns that shape identity and impact. When fear is unconscious, it becomes the default driver. But when it's named, you get your hands back on the wheel.

Let's look at how this played out for three of my clients—each with a different relationship to fear.

▶ RACHEL: Fear as Invisibility

Rachel was a rising leader—smart, capable, and widely respected. When we began coaching, she confessed: "I struggle to own the room." Despite being the most prepared person in nearly every meeting, she often stayed quiet. She'd downplay her expertise or start with disclaimers like, "I'm not sure this is right, but..."

When I asked how she felt in high-stakes settings, she paused. "Exposed," she said. "Like a spotlight is on me, and I want to disappear."

Over time, one thing became clear through our coaching conversations: fear wasn't just a passing emotion—it was an old survival strategy for Rachel. She had grown up in a household where being small and agreeable kept her safe. That pattern had once protected her, but now it was shrinking her leadership.

We worked on this in layers. First, a reframing of her narrative: Fear wasn't a flaw; it was a well-intentioned protector. We practiced grounding techniques to calm her nervous system—breath work, posture, and intentional movement. She experimented with voice and energy work, learning how to speak with warmth and authority. Most important, she practiced visible acts of presence that rewired her fear response: naming her contributions, speaking early in meetings, accepting praise without deflection.

Her turning point arrived during a company-wide talk where she received a standing ovation. But what mattered more was what she told me afterward: "For the first time, I felt like I was fully there—not performing, just present."

Her fear didn't disappear. It just stopped running the show.

► MARCUS: Fear as Emotional Armor

Marcus, a director at a Fortune 100 company, had a reputation for being hard to read. In our first session, he told me, "I'm not political. I just do the work." He was frustrated that despite strong reviews, he kept getting passed over for VP-level roles.

When I conducted his 360-degree feedback interviews,[1] a pattern emerged. Colleagues respected his intellect, but they found him rigid, emotionally unavailable, and disconnected. One said, "It's like talking to a wall. You never know what he's thinking."

In coaching, Marcus revealed a deep fear of being misunderstood. As a first-generation professional from a working-class background, he had masked his insecurities with stoicism. That armor had served him, but now it was a cage. His fear of vulnerability was damaging his leadership brand and potential.

We worked on emotional fluency—expressing thoughts and reactions without self-judgment, opening space for input, and acknowledging when he didn't have the answers. Slowly, people began to see him differently. He earned that promotion, but, more importantly, his team reported higher engagement and trust. They no longer saw him as merely smart and reliable but as a fellow human—someone they could connect with, not just defer to.

---

1 These 360-degree feedback interviews have become a regular feature in many large companies. They are confidential conversations with managers, peers, direct reports, and stakeholders designed to gather broad, honest perspectives about a leader's impact. Coaches are often brought in to conduct the interviews and help employees reach their potential.

► **TAMARA: Fear in a Team Dynamic**

Tamara, a VP leading a high-stakes transformation initiative, couldn't put her finger on what was off. Her team was talented but hesitant. Ideas stalled. Candid conversations were rare.

Through team interviews, I uncovered the issue. Most of the team described the culture as "guarded" and "careful." They respected Tamara but didn't feel safe enough to speak freely. "She always looks so calm and put-together," one said. "It feels like she doesn't need anything from us. So we hold back."

In sessions, I discussed this with Tamara. She was stunned by the feedback. "I thought I was creating psychological safety," she said. But in trying to project unwavering steadiness, she had inadvertently created distance. Her team mistook composure for judgment.

Through our coaching, Tamara began showing more of herself, expressing genuine gratitude, naming tension, and inviting real-time feedback. The energy shifted. Collaboration increased. The team felt safer, not because fear disappeared but because it was acknowledged with intention and care.

These stories don't all look the same on the surface, but they share a common undercurrent.

Fear didn't show up as panic. It showed up as habit. As armor. As silence. And perhaps most of all—it showed up as isolation.

FIELD NOTE: Fear's Favorite Trick—Making You Feel Alone

One of fear's most effective tricks is isolation.

It whispers that you're the only one—the only leader who freezes in meetings, who second-guesses themselves, who feels like an imposter behind a confident mask.

But that's never true. Every leader I've ever coached—from first-time managers to C-suite veterans—has met fear in some form.

What changes isn't the fear itself. It's your relationship to it. When you name it, share it, and work with it instead of against it, fear loses its grip.

Remember this: You're not broken. You're not alone. You're just growing.

The Neuroscience of Fear and Leadership

Fear isn't just emotional—it's biological. When the brain perceives threat, the amygdala kicks in, triggering the fight-flight-freeze response. Useful for survival. Terrible for leadership.

That's because it sidelines the prefrontal cortex, the part of the brain responsible for reasoning, empathy, and executive function. You can't lead from your best self when fear is driving the bus.

In this state, leaders lose nuance. They react, rather than respond. They speak too much or not at all. They default to control, perfectionism, or avoidance.

And fear is sneaky. It wears disguises. One of the most socially acceptable? Overwork.

Many ambitious leaders respond to fear by doubling down. It looks and feels like commitment, but it's often a stress response, rooted in fear of being judged, replaced, or exposed.

Overwork becomes a respectable mask for fear. But it comes at a cost: chronic burnout, trust erosion, and stalled advancement. Leaders who can't delegate or let go rarely scale up—not because they aren't capable but because fear won't let them release control.

One widely seen symptom of fear among high achievers? **Imposter syndrome.** That internal voice that whispers: "You're not as competent as they think. It's only a matter of time before they find out."

A 2020 study found that over 80% of professionals experience imposter syndrome at some point in their careers, including top performers and executives. Imposter syndrome isn't a lack of skill. It's a distortion in self-perception. It's a sign of pressure, visibility, and the relentless drive to prove yourself.

Understanding this helps normalize the experience. Imposter syndrome doesn't mean you are failing. It means you're human—and holding yourself to an impossible standard.

CULTURAL CUE: Gen Z, the New Face of Avoidance

If you lead younger professionals, you may notice that fear takes a different form.

Among Gen Z, fear often looks like avoidance—ghosting conflict, delaying hard conversations, or going quiet when feeling overwhelmed. This isn't flakiness. It's often nervous system overload.

Many Gen Z professionals grew up in hyper-connected environments. They've been digitally documented and publicly judged. For them, visibility often equals vulnerability. For many younger professionals, feedback can feel like surveillance, especially after COVID disrupted early career development. Years of remote work and digital distance created a sense of emotional safety. The subsequent return to in-person observation and real-time evaluation can feel jarring, even exposing.

Avoidance is a signal: "I don't feel safe enough to engage."

The remedy isn't coddling. It's about creating steady ground where younger professionals know they won't be blindsided or judged for learning in real time.

 ## COACHING CUE: Don't Assume Silence
Means Disengagement

Often, it means overwhelm.

The most effective leaders model emotional regulation, deliver feedback with structure, and build psychological safety over time, not just through words but through reliability.

Here are the leadership moves that help Gen Z stay engaged:

- Set clear expectations, and follow through.
- Offer feedback early, privately, and with coaching intent.
- Create opt-in feedback channels, such as Slack surveys and office hours.
- Normalize stress conversations alongside performance goals.
- Model emotional steadiness under pressure. They're watching your nervous system, not just your words.
- Create consistent moments for connection beyond the task because even small rituals matter.

In coaching, I often walk clients through the **Fear-to-Presence Model**—a five-stage progression that helps them move from reactive habits to grounded, intentional leadership. It's not linear, and it's not about perfection. But it offers a powerful map for recognizing when fear is driving the moment and what it takes to return to center. Here's a quick view:

 MODEL: Fear-to-Presence

Each stage is a checkpoint. The goal isn't perfection—it's noticing where you are and what helps you return to presence.

STAGE	DESCRIPTION
REACTING	Fear drives automatic behaviors like overexplaining, micromanaging, or freezing.
AWARENESS	You start noticing patterns without judgment.
REGULATION	You calm your nervous system with breathing, grounding, pausing.
RESONANCE	You reconnect with your values and purpose.
LEADERSHIP	You act from alignment—steady, present, and clear.

COACHING CUE: You Can't Shortcut This Process

Each stage matters, and the more often you walk it, the easier it becomes to return to center.

This chapter lives mostly in the first two stages of the model: **reacting** and **awareness**. What follows is an exploration of how unconscious fear shapes leadership behavior and how bringing it into conscious view is the first step toward presence.

In future chapters, we'll move through the remaining steps—**regulation**, **resonance**, and **leadership**—and show how presence isn't just built but sustained.

FIELD NOTE: Fear Patterns in Leadership

Fear in leadership doesn't always look like panic. Sometimes it shows up in a tailored suit with a polished voice and a calendar full of meetings.

It can show up as:

- **Chronic overwork** driven by the fear of inadequacy
  "If I stay busy enough, no one will question me."

- **Overcontrol or micromanagement** rooted in the fear of being let down
  "I can't trust others to get it right."

- **Avoidance of visibility** tied to the fear of exposure
  "It's safer to stay quiet than risk being wrong in public."

- **Defensiveness when receiving feedback** signaling the fear of being unworthy
  "Any critique equals a threat to my credibility."

- **Fear of being wrong or disagreed with** masked by control or overly justifying
  "If they challenge me, they'll think I don't belong here."

- **Reluctance to delegate** linked to the fear of being judged by others' mistakes
  "If they mess up, it reflects on me."

- **Perfectionism**—driven by the fear of failure
  "If I do it flawlessly, I'll finally feel safe."

Fear doesn't always shout. Sometimes, it whispers in executive language.

But if left unchecked, it quietly writes the rules for how we lead.

COACHING CUE: Watch for Fear That Masquerades as Dedication

Fear often disguises itself as extreme commitment, perfectionism, or loyalty.

But underneath? It's still driving the bus, until you pause, regulate, and reset.

SPIRITUAL CUE: Fear as Shadow

Fear, in its most subtle form, is the shadow of an old self, the version of you that survived through perfection-seeking, silence, or control. It lingers at the edges of your growth, whispering old habits.

But that shadow appears because you're expanding.

If you see fear not as failure but as friction before breakthrough, it becomes a guidepost. You're not going backward—you're growing forward.

In spiritual terms, fear is the final echo of a smaller self that's dissolving. Presence emerges when you stop fighting fear and start walking through it.

READER-TO-LEADER: Reclaiming Presence From Fear

Reflect:

* What is fear trying to protect in you?
* What "old self" does fear still defend?
* Where does fear tend to show up in your leadership behavior? (Overworking? Holding back?)
* When do you feel most present and alive as a leader?

Act:

This week, take one visible step toward presence, even if fear protests:

* Speak first in a meeting.
* Share a bold opinion.
* Ask for feedback.
* Accept praise without deflection.

Presence doesn't begin when fear ends. It begins when you decide to lead anyway.

REMEMBER THIS: *Presence isn't built in a single breakthrough. This work isn't one and done. It's built in layers. In the next chapter, we'll name the blind spots that keep you from being fully seen and begin to dismantle them.*

BLIND SPOTS

The Quiet Sabotage of Executive Presence

You can be brilliant. You can be effective. You can be respected. Still, something you're not aware of in yourself—a blind spot—could be quietly eroding your impact.

Blind spots are not character flaws. They're gaps between how you perceive yourself and how others perceive you. In leadership, those gaps matter more than most people realize, especially in times of disruption, when trust and clarity are in short supply.

Just like driving with part of your side or rear view blocked, blind spots in leadership pose their greatest danger in what you can't see. You may check your mirrors, adjust your lane, and signal carefully—but the real risk comes from the unseen. The higher you rise, the more dangerous that blind spot becomes because the higher you go, the harder it is to get honest feedback. People hesitate. They flatter. They avoid.

Blind spots don't shrink with power. They grow.

The CEO Who Closed His Eyes

I once coached the CEO of a healthcare institution, an exceptionally thoughtful leader, known for his strategic mind, deep curiosity, and appetite for learning. He read books constantly and frequently brought new business ideas to his executive team.

But in important discussions, he had developed a habit: when making a point or responding to questions, he often closed his eyes for extended periods. Not just a blink or two. His eyes would stay shut while he explained a point, pitched a strategy, or gave feedback.

I wondered if it was intentional. It wasn't. In 360-feedback interviews, the eye-closing behavior came up repeatedly. People said it felt like he was retreating or judging them. Some said it made them feel invisible. Others assumed he was disengaged or arrogant.

When I shared this feedback during a coaching session, he paused thoughtfully. "I had no idea," he said. "No one ever told me."

It was as if someone had handed him a mirror he hadn't realized he needed. Rather than getting defensive or retreating further, he became deeply curious about the impact he was having. He leaned into the coaching work with real openness, determined to close the gap between his intentions and the way he was being experienced. Over time, he learned to stay more visibly engaged during conversations, grounding himself with steady eye contact and small physical cues that signaled presence.

The shift was subtle, but powerful—and his team felt it immediately. And the trust that grew from that adjustment wasn't just about optics. It was about emotional accessibility: the quiet message that said, "I'm here with you," not "I'm in my head alone."

To help leaders understand and work with blind spots like these, I often use a classic and powerful tool: the Johari Window.

THE JOHARI WINDOW MODEL
A Fresh Look at Self-Awareness

The Johari Window is a tool developed by two UCLA psychologists to explore how we understand ourselves and how others experience us. It breaks our self-knowledge into four "panes," like a window based on two questions:

- Do I know this about myself?
- Do others know this about me?

Each quadrant represents how information about us flows (or doesn't) between ourselves and others. It includes our behavior, tone, habits, fears, abilities, and even our presence. The difference lies not in what the information is, but in **who** knows it.

In leadership, this matters more than ever. Blind spots that were once minor can be costly in today's disrupted, fast-moving workplaces, where trust and perception are everything.

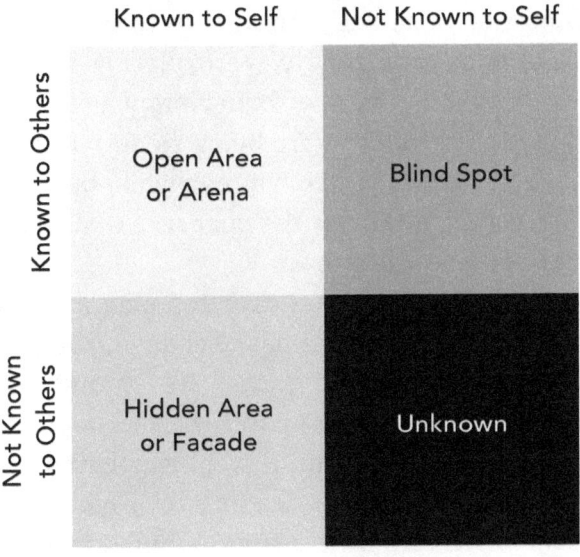

Each pane in the Johari Window graphic (above) reveals something essential.

Quadrant 1
Open area or "Arena" (known to self and others)
This is what you've made visible: your values, leadership style, preferences, and patterns that you and others are aware of. The bigger this window, the more credibility, alignment, and collaboration grow. Teams thrive when leaders are transparent and self-aware.

Quadrant 2:
Hidden area or "Facade" (known to self, not known to others)
This is the private you—the things you choose not to share. Maybe it's vulnerability, past experiences, internal fears, or personal beliefs you keep close. Some of this should stay private. But when leaders never reveal what matters to them, or when they overshare without discernment (especially in today's social media culture), this window stops reflecting reality.

Quadrant 3
Blind area (not known to self, but known to others)
This is the blind spot—the zone we're exploring in this chapter. These are the habits, tone, or behaviors you don't see but others experience. You think you're being clear, but others find you defensive. You believe you're approachable, but your team is afraid to interrupt you. This is the quadrant that shapes your brand, whether you know it or not.

I often say: You can't manage your reputation if you don't know what's in this box. And in times of change, you can't reset your brand without understanding what lies within.

I used to share the following lighthearted example in image consulting training to illustrate this phenomenon: Imagine I dress like I'm twenty-five and heading to a nightclub, but I work in a conservative corporate setting. I think I look amazing. Everyone else is silently wondering, "Why is she wearing that *here?*" That's a blind spot.

Or perhaps it's more serious. I interrupt others constantly and don't realize it. Everyone else feels it, but no one says a word.

Blind spots aren't malicious, but they are expensive.

Quadrant 4
Unknown area (not known to self or others)

This is the most mysterious, and in my view, the most powerful quadrant.

It holds **untapped capacity**: strengths you haven't discovered, instincts you haven't trusted, confidence you haven't claimed. It may also contain repressed fears or unconscious patterns.

But it's not just shadow—it's seed. It's the future you. This is where untapped brilliance and unconscious sabotage coexist. The Unknown Area is why coaching exists, and it's where transformation is hiding.

Many spiritual teachers say the Unknown Self isn't a problem, but rather, an invitation. When we explore what's here, we don't just grow—we remember who we are. We come home to ourselves.

In uncertain times, the Unknown Area also holds resilience. Leaders who are willing to explore what they haven't yet claimed in themselves are better prepared to adapt, reset, and stay grounded when the landscape shifts.

The Johari Window model is powerful in its simplicity. But most leaders underestimate how much of their behavior lives in the Blind and Unknown quadrants. That's where self-awareness becomes more than a buzzword. Let's ground it in what the research says.

FIELD NOTE: The Feedback Gap

A *Harvard Business Review* study found that, while 95% of people believe they are self-aware, only 10%–15% actually are, based on feedback from colleagues and direct reports.

This gap has real consequences for leaders—from misread intentions to missed promotions. But it persists for a simple reason: Most leaders don't get honest feedback. Why not?

- Because of power dynamics.
- Because people don't want to hurt their feelings.
- Because someone already tried, and nothing changed.

And in hybrid or AI-mediated workplaces, feedback is even trickier: people hesitate to put sensitive comments in writing, or they avoid awkward conversations on-screen.

That's why feedback can't be episodic. Make it a leadership discipline—something you normalize, invite, and build into your rhythm.

COACHING CUE: Build a Feedback Rhythm

If you only ask for feedback during performance reviews, you're managing perception reactively, not strategically.
    Try this:

- Ask regularly, not reactively.
- Normalize the request: "What would help me lead better?"
- Go first, then model how you receive feedback.
- Use micro check-ins after meet-ups: "Anything I could improve from that meeting?"
- Reward the honesty, not the delivery.

Don't wait for the calendar to give you permission. Ask in the hallway. After meetings. During key transitions. Treat feedback like vital signs, not a once-a-year diagnostic.

Want to grow? Build a rhythm:

Ask more often.

Receive more openly.

Reflect more honestly.

Feedback isn't something you give or get. It's something you practice routinely and intentionally, even when it's uncomfortable.

It's not a tool. It's a muscle.

Five Blind Spot Profiles

These profiles aren't rare. I see them again and again across industries, levels, and personalities. The patterns repeat. But with awareness, they can shift.

1. The Unseen Leader

"I thought my results would speak for themselves."

These are high performers who avoid visibility. They stay in their lane, assuming their work alone will carry them forward.

Example: Dan, a VP of Operations, had strong metrics and a loyal team. But in enterprise meetings, he barely spoke. He deferred to others. After being passed over for a major promotion, he finally realized his discomfort with visibility was costing him.

We worked on verbal framing, visibility routines, and story-telling. Within six months, he was co-leading strategy sessions and was seen as a peer to the C-suite talent.

Leadership cost: He was perceived as reliable—but not ready for higher visibility roles. His blind spot? Thinking impact was enough without visibility.

2. The Unpolished Leader

"I'm strategic and people-oriented—but they think I look disorganized."

These leaders have presence and instincts, but their image, grooming, or physical presentation unintentionally undercuts their credibility.

Example: Sarah was thoughtful and strategic, deeply respected by her team. But her appearance—sloppy cardigans, chipped nails, worn shoes—sent a different message to senior leaders.

The disconnect undercut her credibility, making her appear far less confident than she truly was. Once she embraced subtle style updates that reflected her capability, her confidence grew—and so did her opportunities.

Leadership cost: She wasn't being underestimated because of her ability but because her image didn't match her potential.

3. The Expert Technical Leader

"I thought expertise was enough."

These professionals lead through mastery rather than influence. They're respected for what they know but limited by how that expertise is received. When credibility depends as much on delivery as content, even small cues can shift perception.

Example: One mid-level auditing professional I coached managed massive portfolios. He was clearly sharp, capable, and committed. But in our first session, I noticed a few recurring grammatical slips in his speech. I made a mental note.

Later, during 360-feedback interviews, a colleague commented that he "often doesn't sound polished" and should avoid presenting externally. When I raised it gently in a later session, the deeper story came out: he had missed most of sixth grade due to a serious car accident and never fully caught up on language instruction. No one had ever told him. He didn't know he was making mistakes.

But that blind spot had held him back in ways he never realized. His leaders valued his technical depth but didn't trust him to represent the company to the outside world.

Once he understood the gap, he committed to coaching and support—not from a place of shame, but clarity. Together, we found targeted language resources online that matched his needs, and he began practicing consistently. Soon he was presenting with confidence, and his opportunities expanded.

Leadership cost: His brand was "sharp but not polished." And he had no idea why.

4. The Unfiltered Leader

"I didn't realize how much my mood shaped the team."

Some leaders don't see how their tone, tension, or volatility sets the emotional climate for everyone around them.

Example: A CMO I coached had no idea that her stress was contagious. She sighed heavily in meetings, went quiet without explanation, and delivered feedback in abrupt bursts. Her team learned to brace themselves. When we gathered feedback, it was clear: her unspoken emotions were running the emotional climate.

Through coaching, she learned to check in with herself before meetings, use emotional transparency, and model self-regulation tools. The change in team energy was immediate.

Leadership cost: She wasn't creating fear intentionally. Her unregulated energy was doing it for her.

5. The Guarded Leader

"I didn't know I was hiding."

These leaders appear composed, even generous, but they are unknowingly playing small, due to old conditioning, fear of arrogance, or cultural programming.

Example: Priya, a senior director, was warm, smart, and trusted. But she constantly downplayed her ideas, overused hedging language ("Just brainstorming here..."), and gave credit away reflexively. She thought she was being collaborative. But to others, it looked like she lacked conviction.

We worked on calm authority, direct language, and visible thought leadership. The shift was subtle but powerful—and people noticed immediately.

Leadership cost: Her ideas were strong, but her delivery made them forgettable.

Blind spots don't just live in client stories. I've had my own, and one of them surfaced in a way I'll never forget.

A Blind Spot of My Own

Most blind spots don't hide in the dramatic. They live in the details—the things no one thinks they can say out loud. Here's a funny (and slightly painful) example from my own life.

Years ago, I was preparing to lead a workshop on business dining etiquette for pharmaceutical reps. The session was set in a fine dining restaurant—multicourse meal, real-time coaching, every detail accounted for.

The day before the training, I was in my home office practicing aloud. My husband popped his head in and said, "Well, just make sure you tell them not to scrape their teeth on their forks." Then he paused. "Actually...honey...you do that. And it really bothers me." I was floored. I had no idea. Apparently, it sounded like nails on a chalkboard to him. And he had waited twelve years to say something.

When I asked why, he said, "I didn't want to hurt your feelings." That's how blind spots work. They live right next to the things people are hesitant to tell you. And they can have a real impact on connection, on perception, and yes, even on dinner. (Also, for those sensitive to sound, this is a real issue. Scraping cutlery can trigger **misophonia**. I had no idea. Now I do.)

Of course, not every blind spot is lighthearted.

REAL TALK: When Coaching Doesn't Work

I've had only two true "failures" in my coaching career—and in both cases, the issue wasn't lack of intelligence or drive. It was an unwillingness to look.

Both clients had been "assigned" coaching. But, in fact, the message was blunter than that; it was more like, "You will not proceed without having a coach." One was a high-level leader with tenure and power, and the other a technical leader respected for output but known for unapproachability. Both were very intelligent. Both were deeply entrenched. And both had blind spots that were widely discussed inside their companies but invisible to them.

In our sessions, every piece of feedback was deflected. Every insight redirected. Every invitation to reflect was met with defensiveness or silence. They didn't want coaching. They wanted out.

Eventually, I told the companies I couldn't continue. Coaching only works if the client is ready to engage. I learned an important truth: you can't make someone want to see what they're not ready to face.

Those blind spots remained because the door was locked from the inside.

Even the most coachable leaders can stall if they're chasing the wrong indicators. Performance might be strong. Metrics solid. And yet, something still doesn't land. Why? Because they haven't been told what actually signals readiness at the next level.

MODEL: The Hidden Job Description

Let me introduce a concept that I believe underlies many executive presence challenges: The Hidden Job Description.

Most leaders don't realize they're working from an incomplete picture. They're doing what's asked. Meeting expectations. Hitting metrics. But they're missing the unwritten rules that determine who gets elevated.

A client once said to me, "I don't get it. I'm delivering everything they asked for." And she was. But the feedback behind closed doors told a different story: she wasn't "showing up like a leader." That gap wasn't about performance. It was about presence.

Here's what I showed her:

STATED ROLE	HIDDEN JOB DESCRIPTION
Deliver results.	Build and manage influence—and ensure the right people know your value.
Manage your team.	Inspire trust across boundaries, including senior and cross-functional leaders.
Communicate information.	Shape perception, calibrate tone, and tune your message to the audience.
Follow the chain of command.	Navigate power dynamics without becoming political.
Perform with consistency.	Project readiness for more—pair productivity with presence.
Stay in your lane.	Think and speak enterprise-wide—proactively advance the business.
Hit your KPIs.	Influence culture, model behavior, and lead through uncertainty.

In today's AI-augmented world, many leaders are managing tasks that machines are already handling faster. But the hidden expectations—presence, influence, discernment—are becoming even more critical. These are the qualities no algorithm can replicate.

When people don't understand this, they pay what I call a **"presence tax":**

- Passed over for promotions without understanding why

- Described as "reliable" but never "transformational"

- Trusted to execute—but not to shape the future

And the worst part? Such professionals never see the receipt. We'll return to this concept in future chapters because so many subtle presence gaps—the ones leaders can't quite figure out— live in the Hidden Job Description.

SPIRITUAL CUE: The Unknown Self

The "Unknown" quadrant of the Johari Window represents what is unknown to both self and others. Most people see this as mysterious or unreachable. But what if it's a place of untapped potential—not something to fear, but something to explore?

The poet Rainer Maria Rilke once advised: "Be patient toward all that is unsolved in your heart and try to love the questions themselves." The unknown is not emptiness. It's possibility.

In leadership, the unknown self is the part of you that hasn't yet been invited forward. The strengths you haven't fully owned. The clarity that emerges only when you're stretched into a bigger version of yourself.

Exploring the unknown isn't about fixing what's missing. It's about trusting that what's hidden may hold the most powerful part of you—if you're willing to meet it with curiosity, not control.

READER-TO-LEADER: Making the Invisible Visible.

Reflect:

- What's one piece of feedback you've avoided, ignored, or rationalized?
- What might be true in it?
- Which of the five blind spot profiles do you most relate to—and why?
- How have your blind spots protected you in the past? Are they still serving you?

Act:

- Ask three trusted colleagues:
  What's one thing I do that strengthens my leadership presence?
  What's one thing I do that might unintentionally undermine it?
- Then: Draft your version of the Hidden Job Description for your current role.
  What's visible? What's essential? What does true readiness look like beyond the metrics?

REMEMBER THIS: *Seeing yourself clearly isn't about being flawless. It's about being free. Because when you make the unconscious conscious, you don't just shift behavior. You reset perception—and identity.*

THE CONFIDENCE ILLUSION

How Presence Is Read

Think about the last meeting you were in. Who looked "confident"? Probably the person who jumped in quickly, spoke without notes, and seemed completely at ease. But was that confidence, or just a deep familiarity with the topic?

Now picture the quieter voice at the table—the person who paused before speaking, or didn't rush to fill the air. We often read that as hesitation, maybe even insecurity. In reality, it might have been thoughtfulness, humility, or simply someone navigating a new level.

Most people have a picture in their head of what confidence looks like: someone who is quick with answers, steady under fire, maybe even a little fearless. But in my work with leaders, I see something different: the most effective leaders don't always rely on inner confidence. They're the ones who know how to be read with credibility. They know how to signal calm authority and intention—even when their insides are churning.

That's what this chapter is about: the illusion of confidence, the signals that get misread, and how to close the gap between what you intend to convey and what others actually experience. Confidence isn't about feeling ready. It's about showing up ready.

And while people judge confidence by what you say or do, something even faster is at work—something others sense before you speak: your energy. Let's unpack what that means.

What Do We Mean By "Energy"?

When I talk about energy in this book, I don't mean your caffeine level. I mean the real, felt impact of how you show up, whether you're speaking or silent, in the room or on a screen. Energy is the atmosphere you create. It's how people feel you before they follow you.

Your energy shows up in your tone of voice, physical presence, attention span, emotional regulation, and even your timing. It can project ease or strain, openness or control, clarity or chaos—sometimes without your being aware of it.

In leadership, energy is not a soft skill. It's a strategic one. It affects how people interpret your decisions, receive your feedback, and trust your leadership. Crucially, in leadership, energy communicates faster than content.

Throughout this book, we'll explore energy from multiple angles—physical, emotional, mental, and spiritual. You'll start to notice patterns in yourself and others. You'll learn to regulate your own energy, read a room, and show up with a clearer, steadier presence.

If the idea of energy feels abstract now, stay with it. We're going to make it very real.

One of the clearest ways I've found to help leaders experience energy—and understand how it's received by others—comes from voice coach Patsy Rodenburg. Her model of the Three Circles of Energy shows why some energy connects—and other energy repels.

📌 MODEL: The Three Circles of Energy

Originally developed for the stage, Patsy Rodenburg's model has helped world-class actors—and now leaders—learn how to project presence that can be felt throughout a room. Her work with the Royal Shakespeare Company, the National Theatre, and iconic performers like Daniel Craig and Ewan McGregor made her one of the most sought-after coaches in the performance world.

But what makes her framework powerful isn't just its theatrical origin: it's how directly it applies to leadership. Many executives have sought her guidance, recognizing that the same principles apply in business. They understand that leadership is shaped by how fully you are *felt* in the room.

Her framework, **The Three Circles of Energy**, offers a simple, practical lens to understand confidence and connection.

The Three Circles

First Circle (Self and Withdrawal): When you're in this circle, your energy collapses inward. You're in your own head, withdrawn and holding back. Others may experience you as hesitant, distracted, or checked out. This isn't "bad"—there are times when it's natural, like when you're working alone, or reflecting. But when you're with others, staying in First Circle means people can't feel you.

Third Circle (Bluff and Force): When you're in this circle, your energy blasts outward in a one-sided way. It can look confident, even "professional," because it's loud and forceful—like a campaign speech at full volume whether or not the audience is with you. Some leaders mistake this for charisma or gravitas. In reality, it's bluff—overbearing and hollow. We've all seen over-talkers who think they're leading when they're really just filling space. This kind of energy pushes *at* people, not with them. Third Circle has its uses in emergencies or moments that demand authority. But as a default, it drains people, shuts down feedback, and weakens connection. Projection isn't presence—people know the difference.

Second Circle (Connection and Presence): In this circle, your energy meets the moment. It's focused, responsive, and relational. You feel fully alive and fully tuned into yourself and to others, listening as well as speaking. This is where trust and influence live.

Rodenburg's goal, especially with actors, was to cultivate a presence so rooted and alive that it could be felt in the back row of a large theater as vividly as in the front. And it wasn't about sheer volume. It was about presence through breath, attention, and emotional connection. She taught actors to drop performance and access something more human: energy that extends not by force but by truth.

For most leaders, Second Circle is not automatic. It takes conscious effort to step into it and even more to stay there. At first, it can feel draining—like learning to use a new muscle that tires quickly. Many leaders slip back into First Circle (withdrawing) or Third Circle (overcompensating) because Second Circle demands presence, focus, and generosity all at once.

But here's the payoff: when you do get into Second Circle and sustain it, everything changes. People listen differently. They trust you more. They open up. They lean in. You become magnetic and genuinely attractive. It pulls people toward you, not because you're louder, but because you're real.

COACHING CUE: Are You in the Second Circle?

Ask yourself:

- Am I meeting the moment or pushing past it?
- Is my energy reaching people or rolling over them?
- Am I trying to control the room or connect with it?

Here's a mantra for recalling this: *Presence that listens and meets.*

In Second Circle, shoulders are open, breath is steady, eyes are curious. You're anchored—aware of yourself but not self-conscious. You meet people without hiding or pushing. The connection is alive, intimate, and human.

Confidence doesn't live in the First or Third Circle. It lives in the Second, where connection grows moment by moment, breath by breath.

► **ANGELA: Transmitting Confidence**

When I first met Angela, she was a strong contender for a VP role at a global food company. Her résumé was stacked with results, but in person she spoke softly, quickly, and almost exclusively in project status updates.

When we debriefed a leadership meeting video I'd asked her to share, she said, "I look terrified. Why am I rushing like that?"

She wasn't terrified. Her energy was stuck in **First Circle**—internal, protective, slightly collapsed. She had always been the high performer behind the scenes, and that habit was spilling into her delivery.

That's when we shifted from mechanics to energy.

We reframed her story from quiet executor to strategic amplifier of the business. We slowed her breathing and her cadence. We helped her voice carry from a steadier place, instead of letting her head race ahead. We encouraged her to let her hands move with purpose.

When Angela shifted into **Second Circle**, the change was real. Her focus stopped scattering and began to land. People described it as if she'd gone from talking *at* them to talking *with* them.

What changed wasn't her résumé. It was her presence. She stopped defending her value and started transmitting it.

Angela's shift was about more than volume or pacing. It was about energy—and it only became clear once the static of fear started to fade. This energetic shift is where real confidence begins. But first, we need to understand what's distorting the signal.

The Static Metaphor: Tuning Out the Interference

Fear is static—not stillness, but the background crackle that scrambles the signal between you and others. Leaders often mistake the static for the message—hearing the inner whisper, "You're not ready... This room is too big for you... They'll see right through you."

But static isn't truth. It's interference. The task is not to erase fear but to tune past it. When the static fades, what comes through isn't louder—it's clearer. That's where confidence begins.

⌕ FIELD NOTE: The Cost of Modesty

Confidence doesn't always look like power poses and polished speeches. Sometimes it's hidden under well-worn habits, like modesty, that limit our visibility even when our work speaks for itself.

I was raised to believe that modesty is a virtue—and it is. But over time, I realized I had internalized a version of modesty. I couldn't accept compliments without deflecting. "It's really nothing," I'd say, or "Anyone could have done it." Even when it *was* something, I couldn't claim it. For years, I mistook self-advocacy for arrogance. Now I know: true presence isn't performance. And owning your strengths doesn't mean abandoning your values.

These days, I keep a sharp eye out for clients who carry that same habit, especially high-performing women and first-generation professionals. We don't throw out their humility. We reframe it.

Modesty without visibility can read as absence. And when your signal doesn't land, neither does your leadership.

COACHING CUE: Reclaim Visibility Without Feeling Fake

If you've been conditioned to downplay your strengths, know this: **perception drives opportunity.** If others can't see your readiness, they won't act on it.

Try this:

- Acknowledge praise graciously. When someone commends you, say: "Thank you. I'm proud of that work."

- Write a credibility story. Capture an achievement that reflects your strengths, then read it aloud. Get used to hearing your own voice speaking about your accomplishments.

- Frame with values. Instead of "Look what I did," try, "This mattered to me, so I made sure it succeeded."

- Catch minimizing language. Ask: "Would I downplay a colleague like this? Why do I do it to myself?"

The Confidence Profiles I See Most

After years of coaching, I've noticed common confidence profiles—all talented, yet all at risk of being misread.

1. The Tentative Striver

The Tentative Striver knows their stuff, but you'd never guess it from the way they show up. They over-edit themselves into invisibility—holding back ideas until they're flawless, second-guessing word choice, or rushing through a point before anyone can react.

Example: Jenna, a senior finance manager, had all the technical chops. But in leadership meetings, she became overly deferential. Her tone was tentative, her eyes scanned for approval, and she often apologized before speaking. She wasn't unsure of her ideas—she was unsure of her right to share them.

Coaching strategy:

- Awareness: We unpacked how her body language echoed her apologize-first posture.

- Practice: I coached her in structured role plays—ending statements with intentional silence instead of another sentence or excuse.

- Anchor phrase: She used, "Here's what I recommend..." to ground her delivery.

- Outcome: Within weeks, Jenna reported, "Colleagues started turning to me in meetings and asking, 'What do you suggest?'" Coaching helped her claim space without waiting for permission.

2. The Presentation-Perfect Performer

The Presentation-Perfect Performer looks like a TED Talk waiting to happen. Their slides are perfect, their image polished, and their delivery carefully rehearsed. They hit all the right notes—but something still feels off. Colleagues sense the show more than the substance.

Example: Anthony, a regional director, dazzled in front of a crowd. Every deck was flawless, every phrase practiced. But after he spoke, his teams didn't engage. Peers felt like he was performing for the room rather than connecting with it. We worked on relaxing his stance, softening his tone, and letting go of the need to impress.

Coaching strategy:

- Live feedback: He brought videos of his presentations, and we reviewed where polish was working against his authenticity and glossing over team contributions.

- Behavioral shift: We integrated directed pauses, such as "What are your thoughts on that?" to invite dialogue.

- Reps: In small team huddles, he practiced unscripted remarks to build trust in his in-the-moment thinking.

- Outcome: He described his next meeting as "the first time it felt like a real conversation, not a presentation."

3. The Quiet Contender

The Quiet Contender has the résumé, the results, and the respect—but hesitates to name their impact. They worry about being seen as self-promotional, so they default to modesty. But in leadership, modesty without ownership creates a vacuum.

Example: Leila, a technical VP, had delivered multiple high-stakes projects. She was trusted and effective, but in cross-functional forums, downplayed her role, deflected praise, and avoided asserting her strategic vision.

"I don't want to seem like I'm taking credit. The team did the work," she said. Once she understood the difference between self-promotion and self-ownership, she began to step forward—and people saw her differently.

Coaching strategy:

- External mirror: I shared what I'd heard from others—that it was her leadership that held those initiatives together. By not naming her role, she was erasing herself from the story.

- Credibility language: We practiced phrases like: "Here's the insight my team brought forward, and the decision I drove based on that."

- Reframe ownership: I reminded her: "You're not erasing your team when you name your leadership. You're modeling it."

- Strategic framing: We worked on showing how her vision connected silos—not as self-promotion, but as enterprise thinking.

At her next cross-functional meeting, Leila opened with, "Let me walk you through what I led, and where we're going next." She didn't change her competence. She changed her stance. And people began to see her as the enterprise leader she needed to be.

4. The Overconfident Operator

The Overconfident Operator speaks with conviction that outpaces their competence. They dominate discussions, weigh in on every decision, or project certainty even when they're not prepared. Charisma may carry them for a while, but over time colleagues begin to doubt the depth behind the bravado.

Example: Darren, a senior sales manager, was quick to speak and decide. Charismatic but overbearing, he often overextended his expertise. His team, weary of his ways, described him as "always certain, not always right."

Coaching strategy:

- Feedback loop: We gathered peer feedback highlighting the gap between Darren's conviction and his follow-through.

- Pause discipline: I coached him to insert a mental checkpoint before weighing in: "Do I have the depth to back this up?"

- Shift focus: Instead of proving himself in every conversation, he began spotlighting his team's expertise.

- Outcome: Darren's credibility rose. He spoke less often, but when he did, people listened—and trusted his judgment more.

FIELD NOTE: The Dunning-Kruger Effect

Darren's story isn't unusual. In coaching, I see both sides of the confidence gap. Some leaders, like Darren, project more certainty than they can back up. Others—often the most capable—downplay their strengths or hesitate to claim their impact.

Psychologists call this the **Dunning-Kruger Effect**, a bias where people with less competence often overestimate themselves, while highly competent people tend to underestimate. This helps explain why some leaders overstate their readiness while equally qualified peers still question if they belong.

I see this often in coaching—some of the most capable leaders doubt themselves the most. Coaching helps reset the gap by restoring alignment between self-perception and reality—grounding confidence in what's real, not exaggerated.

Here's the truth: **you do not have to feel confident to lead**. But you do need to understand how others read you. People infer confidence through tone, body language, and pacing. They trust leaders who speak with clarity, not speed. They read presence through stillness, strategic silence, steady breath, and direct eye contact—not sheer volume.

Research supports this. Harvard's Amy Cuddy showed that even small physical adjustments—like standing in an open posture or taking up more space—can increase your sense of confidence and change how others perceive you. Presence starts in the body, long before your words land.

Understanding how you show up in a room is one part of the work. But to truly shift your presence—especially under pressure—you also need a way to observe yourself in real time. That's where The Witness comes in.

SPIRITUAL CUE: The Witness

The idea of The Witness is ancient—rooted in the Sanskrit word *sakshi*, a central concept in Vedanta. It means "pure observer": the part of awareness that notices thoughts, feelings, and actions without being swept away by them.

Ram Dass helped bring this practice to Western audiences, translating it into simple, practical terms. For him, The Witness wasn't about detachment; it was about presence. It was the ability to notice yourself in real time—to observe with clarity rather than judgment.

The Witness is your inner observer. It's the part of you that can step back and notice, with no judgment, what's happening in the moment. Are you tensing up? Doubting your contribution? Feeling the urge to overexplain or withdraw? When The Witness is present, you don't need to fix anything immediately. You just observe.

You might realize:

"Ah, I'm rushing my words again."

"Interesting. I held my breath when it was my turn to speak."

"There it is, that tightening in my chest when someone interrupts me."

Sometimes, I'll ask clients to imagine their Witness taking a seat above the room like a steady, quiet observer in the corner. This perspective helps reduce emotional reactivity. You are not judging but simply gathering information about yourself. And from that watching, new behavior becomes possible. Over time, this practice builds emotional agility, and with it, composure.

You can't change what you can't see. But once you can see it clearly, it often begins to change on its own.

READER-TO-LEADER: Rethinking Confidence

Reflect:

- Which confidence profile do you slip into the most often?
- When do you notice yourself leaving Second Circle—shrinking back into First or pushing into Third?
- How might observing yourself with The Witness help you return to Second Circle in the moment?

Act:

- Record a short (two to three minutes) video of yourself talking about a topic you know well. Watch it back with curiosity, not critique.
- What energy do you project? What would you shift if you weren't worried about how you came across?
- Practice one small shift this week to bring yourself back to Second Circle.
- Choose one physical anchor to reinforce presence. Lift your posture, breathe low and steady, or let your gaze meet others with curiosity.

REMEMBER THIS: *Confidence grows when you can see yourself clearly and stay present.*

THE UNSPOKEN RULES OF RISING

Why Mastery Isn't Enough

You've mastered the job. But that's not enough. The next leap isn't about performance. It's about presence, influence, and how others experience you as a leader.

Consider Elias's story.

Elias Was Stuck—And He Didn't Know Why

Elias was a high performer in a global supply-chain organization. He had led two massive system implementations, saved the company millions, and consistently received glowing performance reviews. His team was loyal. His outputs were strong. He checked every box, every time.

And yet, when a VP role opened, Elias was passed over.

In our coaching session, he told me, "I have hit every target. I have led flawlessly. What else do they want?" There was no arrogance in his voice—just genuine confusion. Elias thought he'd followed the rules, only to find out there was a second, invisible rule book.

Like many leaders at this level, Elias assumed that doing great work was the ticket upward. And to be fair, it had worked—until now. But the truth is, high performance gets you into the conversation, but it rarely seals the deal.

Over the next few months, Elias began to see what was missing. He wasn't showing up as a peer to his current VPs, he was still behaving like their support system. He rarely spoke in cross-functional meetings unless asked. He delivered updates, not insights. He was more "reliable narrator" than "enterprise visionary." And he didn't cultivate relationships beyond his immediate lane.

His results were great. But his presence didn't signal "ready for more."

Once we started working on what I call the **Hidden Job Description,** everything changed. Elias learned how to shape perception, not just performance. For the first time, Elias understood that leadership readiness isn't just about output. It's a matter of how others read your presence. He became more intentional in meetings, shared bold perspectives, translated data into actionable context, and built trust with senior leaders across the business.

Within a year, he got the promotion. And more important, he understood why.

The Myth of Merit Alone

Many high-achieving professionals believe their work will speak for itself. And to some extent, it does—until it doesn't. At higher levels, expectations shift. Mastery of your current role isn't enough.

The real differentiators become:

- Influence
- Perception
- Strategic presence
- Enterprise thinking

This isn't political. It's practical.

At this level, your scorecard opens the door; your presence decides whether you're invited to stay. People read how you show up—how you hold pressure, how you frame choices, and whether you feel like a peer in the room where decisions are made. It may not feel fair, but it's the real game. Play it with integrity—not manipulation—and you rise.

Earlier, we named the Hidden Job Description. Elias's story brought it to life. This is where we pull it apart so you can see the patterns and apply them yourself.

MODEL: The Hidden Job Description

Every leadership role has two layers:

- The stated role: The official job description as it was posted, recruited for, and measured against, usually focused on deliverables, metrics, and scope of control
- The Hidden Job Description: Energy, influence, perception, political acumen, enterprise thinking

The Hidden Job Description is often invisible because no one teaches it. It's passed along in whispers. Observed, not explained. But once you learn to spot the patterns, you can lead with more intention and accelerate your rise.

This is what I show clients when they feel stuck—not due to performance but because they haven't been told what presence and leadership look like at the next level.

How do these hidden expectations show up in everyday leadership goals? Let's break it down.

The Hidden Job Description in Action

IF YOU'RE AIMING TO...	DON'T JUST...	ALSO START TO...
Move from execution to enterprise scope	Execute flawlessly	Speak in terms of business outcomes, connect work to larger strategy.
Be seen as a peer to senior leaders	Share updates in meetings	Offer perspective, show original thinking, ask smart questions.
Get promoted to VP	Hit all your KPIs	Build relationships with decision-makers, show readiness, own a bigger narrative.
Lead through change	Manage deliverables	Inspire confidence, communicate clearly, stay calm under pressure.
Influence cross-functional priorities	Stay in your lane	Build coalitions, anticipate objections, tailor your message for different leaders.

COACHING CUE: Visibility is a Leadership Behavior

If no one sees your readiness, they can't act on it. Visibility isn't self-promotion—it's stewardship. When you share your work, you make it easier for others to trust, include, and sponsor you.

The Hidden Job Description Changes by Industry

Let's be honest—no one hands you a memo called "How to Get Promoted." But there is one and it's hidden in plain sight.

While the gap between formal job requirements and hidden expectations exists across organizations, the specific elements of the Hidden Job Description vary dramatically by industry, culture, and context.

Tech Leadership: The Innovation-Execution Paradox

In high-growth technology companies, the Hidden Job Description often revolves around balancing seemingly contradictory expectations:

STATED ROLE	HIDDEN JOB DESCRIPTION
Drive innovation and "move fast"	Deliver scalable results that align with business priorities.
Be technically credible	Translate technical complexity into clear strategic context.
Manage agile teams	Push teams past comfort toward growth.
Collaborate cross-functionally	Influence without authority to move work forward.
Deliver results	Build the bench that makes results sustainable.

Here's how that paradox plays out in practice.

Sophia, a VP of engineering at an AI-focused startup, faced these tensions daily. She was brought in for her technical brilliance and product vision. But six months in, her CEO pulled her aside:

"The team loves your ideas, but they need more than inspiration. They need structure," he told her.

In coaching, we uncovered that she wasn't failing. She was simply emphasizing one side of her role at the expense of the other. Her Hidden Job Description required balancing a polarity that wasn't explicitly named in her job spec: disrupt and deliver, innovate and implement.

Once she recognized this invisible expectation, she began consciously balancing her leadership approach—still championing bold ideas but pairing them with clear execution frameworks.

Financial Services: The Risk-Growth Tension

In financial institutions, the Hidden Job Description takes a different shape, often centering on these tensions:

STATED ROLE	HIDDEN JOB DESCRIPTION
Manage risk and ensure compliance	Find creative paths to growth within constraints.
Follow established processes	Modernize systems without disruption.
Uphold institutional stability	Drive change and digital evolution.
Maintain client relationships	Expand service offerings and revenue.
Optimize current operations	Prepare for industry transformation.

James, an SVP at a global bank, was renowned for his risk management expertise. But despite his technical excellence, he kept getting passed over for C-suite roles.

When we dug deeper, we discovered the missing piece: while he excelled at identifying risks, he rarely proposed solutions. He was seen as the leader who found problems, not the one who creatively navigated through them.

His Hidden Job Description required not just risk identification but risk navigation—finding the path through constraints rather than simply highlighting them.

Healthcare Leadership: The Care-Cost Balance

In healthcare organizations, leaders navigate perhaps the most complex Hidden Job Description of all.

STATED ROLE	HIDDEN JOB DESCRIPTION
Deliver quality patient care	Optimize operational efficiency.
Manage clinical teams	Influence physicians who don't report to you.
Meet regulatory requirements	Drive innovation within compliance.
Control costs	Invest in future capabilities.
Focus on patient experience	Balance staff well-being and burnout.

 COACHING CUE: Owning Your Hidden Job Description

The Hidden Job Description operates at every level. Industries have unspoken expectations shaped by market pace and norms—what signals readiness in tech might look very different in healthcare or finance. Organizations layer on their own unwritten codes: who gets airtime, how decisions get made, what kind of visibility earns trust. At the personal level, your Hidden Job Description is the **distinct set of expectations others hold of you**—shaped by your role, stakeholders, history, and context.

Seeing all three levels clearly helps you lead with intention instead of guesswork. The next exercise will help you surface those expectations and translate them into practical insight you can act on right away.

The Four-Question Discovery Process

I've developed a straightforward approach to help executives uncover their own Hidden Job Description. It involves asking four questions of the right people:

1. **What do successful leaders at my level do that isn't in any job description?**
   Ask peers who have successfully navigated your organization or industry.

2. **What might be holding me back that I don't see?**
    Ask trusted mentors or coaches who can provide unfiltered feedback.

3. **What do you need from me that you're not explicitly asking for?**
    Ask both your boss and your direct reports. Their answers will often differ dramatically.

4. **What's changing in our industry or organization that's not yet reflected in how we evaluate leadership?**
    Ask forward-thinking colleagues and industry connections.

One client, Nina, a Regional Director at a consumer packaged-goods company, used this process in coaching to recalibrate how she showed up and what she prioritized.

Her boss revealed that while hitting sales targets was table stakes, what truly differentiated top performers was their influence across functions, especially in marketing and product development.

This had never come up in their formal check-ins or performance reviews, but it was a quiet make-or-break expectation. Once she heard it, it explained a lot.

Her peers shared that the most successful regional directors weren't just executing corporate strategy. They were actively contributing to it by identifying local market trends that could scale nationally.

Her direct reports admitted they didn't need more direction. They needed **the why**—context, purpose, and connection to the bigger picture.

And a former mentor reminded her that sustainability and purpose-driven initiatives were becoming critical leadership competencies, even though they weren't yet part of formal evaluations.

From these conversations, Nina didn't just collect feedback. She built a blueprint.

She stopped chasing every expectation equally and started leading with clarity. Her personal Hidden Job Description became a compass for where to invest her time, how to shape perception, and how to align her strengths with what the business valued.

She didn't just learn what was missing. She learned how to lead with it.

COACHING CUE: Ask the Right Questions

Leaders who rise don't wait for someone to spell out expectations—they ask. And when they do, it signals more than curiosity. It shows humility, courage, and enterprise thinking.

The willingness to ask—and to really hear what others may not say—isn't just a tactic. It's a leadership behavior.

Uncovering your Hidden Job Description is only half the work. In today's hybrid world, the bigger challenge is making your presence visible across rooms, platforms, and screens.

The Visibility Revolution: How Digital has Changed the Game

It's not just about being in the room anymore. It's about being visible across the business—in conversations you're not part of, on platforms you don't control, and in digital spaces that never sleep.

Executive visibility isn't what it used to be. It's no longer built only through office presence and hallway conversations. Today, your influence often begins long before you enter the room—and it continues long after you've logged off.

FIELD NOTE: The Evolution of Executive Visibility

TRADITIONAL VISIBILITY	DIGITAL-ERA VISIBILITY
Limited to physical presence in key meetings	Extends across platforms, time zones, and formats
Restricted to formal communication channels	Includes thought leadership, social engagement, virtual presence
Measured by those you know personally	Includes network reach and digital influence
Built through hierarchical advancement	Can be built through lateral visibility and online thought leadership
Controlled and contained	More transparent and permanent

Your leadership signal now travels through more channels than ever—and each one shapes your reputation.

Increasingly, your digital presence isn't just a supplement—it's a starting point. Colleagues, clients, and decision-makers may experience your leadership online before they ever meet you in person. LinkedIn posts, Slack replies, internal emails: they all contribute to the narrative of who you are.

But it's not just your ideas or status updates that get noticed. It's your tone, energy, and emotional openness. And the leaders who understand this shift are the ones who stand out. Maya's story shows what that looks like in practice.

► MAYA: Digital Leadership Pivot

Maya, a sharp and strategic CFO at a midsize manufacturing company, was respected for her financial acumen but struggling to gain enterprise-wide influence. In her organization, visibility had traditionally been established through decades of relationship building and physical presence at headquarters. But that model was changing. Visibility was no longer defined only by who you knew in the halls—it was increasingly shaped online.

And online, what mattered wasn't just participation but tone: the openness, accessibility, and emotional signal you conveyed in online interactions.

Maya was making an impact, but under these new rules of visibility, much of it went unseen. She grew frustrated—not because her work lacked value, but because the executive team couldn't see it.

As a newer leader based in a regional office, Maya recognized an opportunity in the digital shift. She began strategically expanding her visibility, not through performative posting but through meaningful contribution:

- She set up virtual "open office hours"—a scalable, low-lift way to invite finance questions from any department.

- She created bite-size explanations of complex financial concepts for the company intranet.

- She participated actively in cross-functional Slack channels, offering financial perspective when it helped others move forward.

In short, Maya didn't rely on outdated models of visibility. She shifted the terms to match her strengths.

Within six months, Maya's influence had expanded dramatically, not by performing louder, but by showing up in ways that reflected her authentic style and context.

Maya's story is one example of a larger shift: visibility no longer depends on proximity. It now depends on how far your presence travels.

COACHING CUE: Rethink How You Get Seen

In today's hybrid world, showing up doesn't always mean being in the room. Maya didn't work harder or speak louder—she changed *how* she showed up.

Visibility today includes asynchronous tools, digital channels, and informal influence, from Slack and email to thought leadership and executive summaries.

You don't need to be everywhere. But you do need to be seen in the spaces where decisions are shaped.

🔍 FIELD NOTE: The New Hidden Expectations

Today's leadership landscape includes a wave of unspoken expectations that didn't exist even five years ago. You're not just being evaluated on presence in the room, but across platforms, contexts, and cultures. These are now part of the Hidden Job Description for modern leadership:

- **Digital fluency.** Moving fluidly between in-person and virtual settings with clarity, confidence, and professionalism.

- **Content creation.** Turning your expertise into shareable, strategic insights that reflect strategic thinking and value-add beyond your lane.

- **Omni-channel presence.** Showing up consistently across internal and external platforms, such as emails, meetings, Slack, LinkedIn, TikTok, Zoom, and more.

- **Asynchronous influence.** Making an impact when you're not in the room means communicating through written updates, recorded messages, and informal leadership signals that travel without you.

- **Digital emotional intelligence.** Reading tone, energy, and interpersonal cues across screens. Consider how delays, punctuation, or brief replies might be interpreted by others.

- **AI-aware leadership.** Understanding what technology can streamline and what only human leadership can perform. Presence, discernment, and relational depth are no longer extras. They're your edge.

Like it or not, your digital trail is now part of your leadership brand. People are watching, scanning, and drawing conclusions. Here's how your boss and other decision-makers are interpreting those cues.

 COACHING CUE: What Your Boss Is Really Watching

Most rising leaders underestimate just how closely their everyday behaviors are being scanned for signals of executive readiness. Your boss isn't just tracking results. They're reading the subtler cues:

- Do peers seek you out or avoid you?
- Do you lead meetings with clarity, or just report status?
- Do you provide insights, or simply deliver data?
- Do you act like a peer, or wait for permission to contribute?

These aren't soft skills. They're the signals leaders use to decide who's ready for bigger scope.

And while those patterns build over time, one moment shapes how you're seen most powerfully: the first impression.

The Power of First Impressions

Let's be clear: First impressions[2] aren't everything. **But they're close.**

According to a Princeton University study, people form judgments about someone's trustworthiness, competence, and likability within the first **1/10th of a second.** Once formed, they're incredibly sticky. They shape how just about everything that follows will be perceived.

When I moved from finance into image consulting, this insight

---

2 For more information on first impressions, check out Appendix II at the back of the book.

changed everything. I began coaching leaders who had the talent but hadn't yet aligned their visual or energetic presence with their ambition. Today, I still share this data in executive sessions because it remains one of the most powerful and most ignored drivers of perception.

Here's why it matters so much: Harvard Business School professor Amy Cuddy's research reveals that when people assess others, they're making two primary evaluations:

Warmth: Can I trust you?

Competence: Can you lead me?

These assessments often happen **unconsciously,** and once formed, they shape how everything you say or do is filtered.

Whether you're walking into a boardroom, logging onto Zoom, or introducing yourself to a cross-functional team, your presence is already speaking. Posture, grooming, expression, attire, tone—these aren't superficial. They're signalers. And they influence whether people see you as credible, relatable, or both.

COACHING INSIGHT: Professional Does Not Mean Stiff

Not long ago, "professional" meant one narrow look: pressed suits, polished shoes, and strict dress codes with very little room for individuality. Today's standards have widened. Cultural, racial, gender, and generational expressions all shape how leaders show up. I embrace that broader lens. But presence still signals readiness, and appearance still communicates credibility.

That's why I bring clients back to three core questions:

- Does your appearance match the level you want to lead at?

- Is your look helping or hurting the credibility of your message?

- What first impression are you making before you even speak?

You don't have to be conventionally attractive or dressed in designer clothes. But you do need to look like you belong at the level you're leading. That's what style signals, and it's within your control.

Perception Is Part of the Job

Let's put this plainly: **If your leadership isn't visible, it isn't effective.**

Managing perception isn't about spin—it's about clarity. You can have the right skills, ideas, and intent, but if others can't see them, they can't trust that these qualities exist. Perception shapes opportunity because it signals readiness.

Here's what perception management looks like in action:

- Tailoring communication to the audience without losing authenticity
- Balancing humility with assertion
- Showing up composed and prepared, especially under pressure
- Reading the room and adjusting in real time

When Perception Breaks Across Generations

I see this all the time in coaching, not just at the VP level, but across the entire leadership arc. A leader is showing up with heart, effort, and capability, and still getting misread. Not because they're unqualified. Not because others are resistant. But because their presence hasn't been translated across generational lines.

Younger leaders often bring emotional openness, authenticity, and purpose. Senior leaders may still value polish, brevity, and visible decisiveness. The result isn't a merit problem—it's a perception problem. Signals get crossed. Intentions get lost.

Younger leaders often fear being perceived as too casual or emotional. Older leaders may feel overlooked or outdated. But both are often misreading one another's intent. And trust can quietly erode before anyone names the gap.

You don't need to become someone else. But you do need to understand the system you're operating in and learn how to bridge your personal style with the cues that still carry weight in executive culture.

This isn't just a personal challenge. It's a cultural one. And if left unspoken, it begins to fray the fabric of leadership cultures inside organizations.

Generational Differences Don't Equal Cultural Drift

Much has been written about generational divides—Boomers, Gen X, Millennials, Gen Z—as if the differences themselves are the problem. But the real risk isn't difference—it's disconnection. Leaders retreat into their age cohort. Teams interpret each other through outdated assumptions. Trust erodes not because of values but because no one is translating.

Here's what I often see in coaching:

- Millennial leaders may feel they've earned a seat through collaboration, inclusion, and tireless effort. Yet they're often told they need to "show more gravitas" in executive rooms.

- Gen Z professionals bring transparency, boldness, and emotional fluency. But then find themselves misunderstood as "immature" or "too casual."

- Gen X and Boomers sometimes feel dismissed or sidelined by a wave of tech-driven change, even when they're still driving business-critical results and mentoring rising talent.

- Across all generations, there are leaders quietly asking: "Do they see me? Do I still belong here?"

These moments don't stem from malice. They stem from a mismatch between style and expectation, values and visibility. That's where leadership comes in. Your job isn't to erase differences. It's to **anchor them back to shared purpose**.

Great leaders don't just tolerate generational differences. They build cultures that integrate them. They connect individual styles to team values. They stay curious about what they don't yet understand. And they create systems that honor different ways of communicating without fragmenting accountability.

When you do that, you stop disconnection before it starts. You build a culture where every generation feels part of the mission, not just a product of their age group.

Here's what it looks like when a leader chooses to translate rather than dismiss.

► MATT: Translating Boldness Into Belonging

Matt, a Senior Manager in supply chain, was initially frustrated by a Gen Z analyst who challenged priorities during a planning meeting. His gut reaction? "That's out of line."

But then Matt paused. He reminded himself: boldness was one of the company's stated values.

The analyst's challenge was actually an expression of the company's value of boldness—albeit in unpolished form.

Instead of correcting him, Matt coached him on how to frame disagreement for impact. The result? A stronger connection to company values through clarity, not conformity.

FIELD NOTE: Leading Across Generational Lines

FOCUS POINT	LEADERSHIP MOVE
Different work styles	Connect them to a shared mission and impact.
Different communication modes	Create flexible but clear expectations.
Different career timelines	Normalize varied growth paths, without judgment.
Different values around balance	Frame well-being and flexibility as leadership levers—not liabilities.

 COACHING CUE: For Next-Gen Leaders Navigating Perception

Leadership is culture work. Every generation can strengthen culture, or quietly fracture it. If you're navigating the friction between authenticity and expectation, remember: leading across generations isn't just about adapting your style. It's about how you connect individual expression to collective culture.

- How can I signal confidence without abandoning vulnerability?

- What executive behaviors could I adopt without feeling fake?

- Where might structure free me and not constrain me?

You don't have to lose your voice to grow your presence. But you do have to lead with clarity inside the system you're trying to shape.

SPIRITUAL CUE: Sacred Ambition

Medieval mystic Meister Eckhart taught that desire itself isn't the problem—attachment is. You can want to rise. You can work to be seen. You can honor your ambition as sacred, not shameful.

The test: Can you hold your goals lightly? Can you pursue visibility while remaining unshaken if recognition doesn't come?

Thomas Merton wrote: "The beginning of love is to let those we love be perfectly themselves, and not to twist them to fit our own image." The same applies to yourself. Don't twist yourself into the image of "executive-ready" so completely that you lose your essence.

The Hidden Job Description is real. The unspoken rules matter. Master them with integrity. Rise with intention.

Just don't confuse climbing the ladder with being whole.

Your ambition can be sacred when it serves something larger than status. When it creates space for others to rise. When it refuses to abandon your values for a seat at the table.

Master the game. Just remember: the unspoken rules don't define you—they reveal where you choose to show up.

READER-TO-LEADER: Executive Readiness, Reframed

Reflect:

- Are you over-relying on performance to carry your career?
- What signals are you unintentionally sending in high-stakes settings?
- Where are generational or style differences affecting how you're read?
- Where am I unintentionally expecting others to match my style, instead of building cultural bridges?
- Which part of the Hidden Job Description have you ignored—profile, voice, or relationships?

- How do you come across in exec-level rooms? (Ask a trusted peer.)

Act:

- In your next high-visibility meeting, offer a strategic perspective, not just an update.

- Strengthen your cross-functional presence: reach out to a peer in another part of the business and exchange insights.

- Audit your digital presence—LinkedIn, Zoom, Slack, intranet, email tone. What do these channels say about your leadership?

- Ask one person from your leadership team, your peers, and your direct reports: "What's one thing I could do differently to show I'm ready for the next level?" Write down their answers without defending yourself.

> **REMEMBER THIS:** *Rising isn't just about results. It's about credibility, visibility, and the presence that quietly shapes opportunity.*

LEADING ACROSS

Power, Trust, and the Politics of Peers

From what I've seen in coaching, the hardest leadership isn't always managing up or down. It's sideways. Peer dynamics often create the biggest friction—and the biggest breakthroughs.

Managing sideways means managing your peers: the people who don't report to you. The ones who sit beside you in meetings. The ones who might one day be your boss or your direct report. The ones who got promoted instead of you. Or didn't—and now you're their manager.

Peer dynamics are the quiet theater of leadership maturity—rarely discussed, but constantly shaping outcomes.

The Shifting Nature of Peers

Here's the hard truth: Your peers won't stay peers forever. In a high-performing environment, someone gets promoted. Someone else doesn't. Someone's scope expands. Another person gets reassigned. Today's collaboration is tomorrow's power imbalance, or vice versa.

And when that happens? Unspoken emotions like these often surface:

- Jealousy

- Grief

- Competition

- Guilt

- Distance

- Resentment

These are very human emotions—and not to be minimized. If you don't name them, they run the show underneath the surface.

COACHING INSIGHT: When Peers Become Unequal

Jasmine and Nadia had grown up in the company together. Hired the same year. Promoted within weeks of each other. They joked that they were "co-pilots"—different functions but the same meetings, work ethic, and rhythm.

Then Jasmine got the big promotion. Vice President. Nadia, however, did not.

"She smiled," Jasmine told me in a session, "but then she stopped talking to me. Just enough that I felt it."

It wasn't sabotage or drama. It was withdrawal.

In coaching, Jasmine explored her own discomfort, too. There was guilt about rising, fear of losing connection, a desire to stay peer-like, even though the power dynamic had shifted.

Together, we crafted a reset conversation:

"I value our history more than you know. I also realize this change may be harder than either of us expected. I want us to find a way to keep showing up strong—whatever that looks like now."

Nadia responded. Slowly. But it reopened the door.

Leadership requires grace in proximity—knowing when to invite closeness, when to name tension, and when to rebuild once the power tilts.

Common Peer Dynamics

Here are the patterns I see most often in coaching:

- The loyal ally: A peer who roots for you, even when you're rising
- The friendly competitor: Someone supportive on the surface, but quietly keeping score
- The bystander: The person who observes your struggles or successes without engagement
- The resentful former peer: A coworker who struggles to respect your role after a promotion
- The ghost: This colleague congratulates you, then withdraws
- The spotlight sharer: They publicly affirm your work but subtly redirect credit in strategic rooms

These patterns aren't inherently toxic, but they carry emotional weight. Naming them is the first step toward leading across them.

COACHING CUE: The Fairness Fantasy

Peer tension often emerges from what I call the **fairness fantasy**, the quiet belief that if everyone works hard, stays in sync, and plays by the same rules, recognition will be shared equally.

But promotions don't follow emotional contracts. When one person rises faster than expected, it disrupts that illusion, and what surfaces is not always envy, but a sense of emotional asymmetry. Someone broke the rhythm. And even when that rise is earned, it can leave others feeling exposed, left behind, or quietly resentful.

The key is to see this clearly and respond with maturity rather than guilt or avoidance.

What we believe about fairness and recognition isn't just personal. It's shaped by deeper group dynamics, power cues, and trust patterns. Here's what the emerging research suggests about peer dynamics in practice.

Research Note: What We Know (And What We Don't)

Formal research on peer dynamics in leadership is still emerging. But for now, this is what we know:

- Center for Creative Leadership found that strong peer networks are a major predictor of long-term leadership success, especially in flat or matrixed organizations.

- Amy Edmondson's research shows that psychological safety among peers directly impacts trust, risk-taking, and collaboration.

Many organizations already invest in team dynamics workshops or use assessments like DISC to map different behavioral styles. These tools can be very helpful in improving communication, collaboration, and conflict resolution. They show that peer dynamics are on the radar inside companies.

But here's the gap: a workshop or assessment can only take you so far. What's missing in the research is what leaders actually live: the strain when one person gets promoted, the resentment when fairness feels off, and the distance that grows when peers stop talking.

Again and again, I've seen one factor make or break peer dynamics: whether people feel safe enough to be honest.

COACHING CUE: Psychological Safety Among Peers

Peer safety isn't about comfort. It's about knowing you won't be punished, socially or politically, for offering an honest view. Peers create safety by following through, listening without penalty, and making room for ideas that challenge their own. Safety matters even more when authority is diffuse, and influence has to travel sideways.

FRAMEWORK: Leading Across a Matrix

In matrixed organizations, peer dynamics become even more complex. You're often expected to lead through influence—not title. These relationships are messy. No one reports to you. You can't compel compliance. But you're still accountable for results.

To lead across a matrix, you need three things:

- **Presence over pressure**
  People don't follow command-and-control in matrix systems. They follow steadiness. When you show up with emotional regulation, clarity, and strategic framing—peers lean in. Presence is reinforced by follow-through; visible accountability builds trust and momentum.

- **Shared purpose framing**
  In misaligned systems, tension rises fast. Instead of proving your side, try naming a shared goal: "We're coming at this from different angles, but we're solving for the same customer."

  Name the purpose early and clearly. It resets the tone and keeps peers aligned.

- **Pre-alignment rituals**
  Don't wing high-stakes meetings with matrix partners. Five minutes of pre-check can prevent a week of cleanup:
  "Here's what I'm planning to say—are we good?"
  "Any risks you want me to be mindful of in that room?"

These rituals, paired with steady reminders (not pressure), keep shared goals on track. Elevate peers in rooms they aren't in, and engage senior stakeholders when alignment is needed across lanes.

These strategies land best when delivered from Second Circle—grounded, attuned, and relational. Matrix leadership is about resonating in a way that others choose to follow. But even when you show up well, fractures still happen. When alignment breaks, the reset matters.

The Peer Rift and the Reset

Lena was a director of digital product. Her peer Cory was in design. For two years, they partnered tightly—shared late nights, co-led launches, and traded high fives in Slack.

Then Lena was promoted to lead a strategic initiative. Cory wasn't.

He started missing meetings, ghosted a deadline, and held back on collaboration. Lena felt it.

We worked through a non-blaming reset. She met him one-on-one, saying:

"Cory, I've sensed a shift. If I've contributed to that—even unintentionally—I want to name it. I value what we've built, and I want to keep working with clarity and respect."

He didn't rush to reassure her. But he softened. He shared his disappointment, not in her, but in himself. And the air started to clear.

Sometimes peer repair doesn't require a deep apology. Just the willingness to name what's happening.

Not every leader takes the coaching. One VP client—let's call her Tasha—experienced a similar peer freeze after her promotion. She sensed the tension but avoided it. "I don't want to make it worse," she said. She thought it would blow over. But it didn't.

Six months later, a key cross-functional project went sideways. Her former peer withheld critical context in a partner meeting—not out of sabotage but disengagement. Tasha's credibility took a hit.

She didn't fail because of any lack of skill. Tasha failed because silence calcified into distance.

The lesson: Peer dynamics don't reset themselves. Leaders do.

FIELD NOTE: When Favoritism Tilts the Room

Sometimes, peer dynamics fracture because one person becomes "the favorite"—the boss's go-to, the one who dominates meetings, the one with constant airtime. Whether deserved or not, it creates imbalance.

Peers won't always name this tension out loud. But they feel it. And if left unchecked, it erodes collaboration.

If you sense that pattern forming around you, interrupt it early and visibly.

- Say: "I notice we've heard a lot from a few voices. I'd like to open the floor—what other perspectives are we missing?"
- Watch who gets praised publicly and who never gets mentioned.
- Make space. Then redistribute it.

Favoritism isn't always intentional. But its impact always is.

► DEREK: Leading Without the Title

Not all peer influence comes through role or hierarchy. Some of the most powerful shifts I've seen start from presence alone. Derek was a senior program manager in a global retail organization. No direct reports. No formal authority. But everyone in his ecosystem came to him first. Why?

Because he brought clarity, framed strategy, and elevated others.

When a senior executive finally asked him to co-lead a major cross-functional launch, Derek said, "But I don't have the title."

The exec replied: "You already lead the work. Let's just make it official."

Influence doesn't begin with power. It begins with resonance. And that's where a practical tool can help you see your own influence more clearly.

TOOL: The Peer Influence Web

Put yourself at the center of a page and jot your peers' names around you in a simple web. Then ask yourself four questions as you map:

- **Clarity.** Who understands the impact of my work, and who doesn't?

- **Support.** Who would vouch for me when I'm not in the room?

- **Strain.** Where do I feel distance, drift, or quiet resistance?

- **Equity.** Where have I invested without expecting something back?

Once your map is on paper, choose one move this week:

- Clarify your kinship with someone who doesn't fully support you.

- Repair a strained relationship before silence hardens.

- Amplify a peer who could use visible support.

When one client sketched hers, she realized she'd invested 80% of her relational energy in peers she liked rather than peers she needed to influence. That single insight reframed how she spent her time and attention — and within months, her peer credibility doubled.

A map can show you where your influence is strong and where it's thin. But seeing the web is only step one. Repairing and renewing those connections is where the work begins.

Repair Is Part of the Work

I've coached many leaders who were deeply trusted by senior executives. They had access, credibility, and a strong track record. But among peers? The picture was different.

One client, a VP of strategy, had built strong relationships at the C-suite level. She was known for delivering under pressure and being "the one to call" for critical initiatives. But her peers often felt excluded or disempowered. In coaching sessions, she described them as resistant, withholding, even undermining.

What she hadn't realized was that her proximity to power had created distance on the horizontal plane. She was seen as "too inside," or worse, someone who couldn't be fully trusted. No one had ever told her that directly. But she could feel it in the silence, the lack of support, the subtle ways peers avoided collaboration.

We worked on resetting those relationships—not from apology, but from presence. She began acknowledging shared goals, inviting peers into upstream conversations, and naming unspoken tensions with calm transparency. The shift was powerful. The more she owned her impact, the more peers leaned back in.

Sometimes the relationship itself doesn't need to be rebuilt. But the perception around it does.

 COACHING CUE: Relational Ecosystem

Most rising leaders manage up and down to their boss and to their team. But the ones who accelerate manage *across*—on purpose.

Your peer relationships are personal *and* strategic. They shape how fast your ideas move, how others sponsor your work, and how much informal influence you carry.

Run your ecosystem with a simple cadence:

- Sponsor laterally. Name a peer's contribution in a room they're not in. Make it visible without keeping score.

- Repair early. When energy drags, reach out: "Noticed some friction—can we reset?" Small resets prevent big rifts.

- Practice generosity. Offer context, connections, or credit without expecting return. It strengthens the soil.

- Ask directly about friction. A simple: "What would make working with me easier?" can draw out what the silence has hidden.

SPIRITUAL CUE: Leadership Without Attachment

In Buddhist teachings, there is a concept called *mudita*—the practice of feeling joy for others' success, even when their win is not your own.

It is the opposite of envy. It's a muscle that strengthens generosity and a test of whether your leadership is performative or truly embodied.

The Bhagavad Gita teaches us to act from alignment, with full presence but without attachment to recognition or reward. When applied to leadership, this means showing up with care and steadiness, even when the outcome feels unfair or unseen.

Together, these traditions invite a powerful shift:

Lead with clarity, not comparison.

Celebrate without calculation.

Influence without control.

Your leadership isn't diminished by another's rise. It's revealed in how you respond to it.

READER-TO-LEADER: Influence Among Equals

Reflect:

- Who are the five people beside you in your organization—not above or below—who influence your path?
- Which peer relationship could benefit from more clarity, care, or calibration?
- Where could you extend acknowledgment, repair, or generosity?

Act:

- Have one clarity conversation with a peer this week.
- Publicly acknowledge a peer's contribution in a group setting.
- Help someone not because they're "in your lane" but because you can.

> **REMEMBER THIS:** *Peer dynamics live in the middle—the space without hierarchy, but full of impact. And the way you show up there speaks volumes about your maturity as a leader.*

THE ENERGY SHIFT

How Leaders Build Staying Power

Most leaders are taught to push harder, dig deeper, and out-work everyone else. That may get you through a sprint, but it doesn't create staying power.

In today's turbulent times, stamina alone won't carry you. Leadership isn't about sheer endurance, but instead, a rhythm of effort, recovery, and renewal. It's how you manage your energy—physical, emotional, mental, and spiritual. That's the shift this chapter is about.

Amira Was Burning Out—And No One Could Tell

Amira had just been promoted to SVP of Operations at a fast-scaling consumer technology company. Her reputation inside the organization was near-mythic: unflappable under pressure, responsive at all hours, a master of making the impossible happen with limited resources.

She was the person everyone counted on. In meetings, she

always had the answer. Her emails came at 10 p.m., and responses were expected. She didn't complain. She just delivered.

This is precisely what made her promotion feel like both a reward and a trap.

When she came into our coaching engagement, she looked like someone who hadn't taken a deep breath in months. Her tone was polished, her pace relentless. But her face told a different story.

"I'm proud of how far I've come," she said quietly. "But I'm not sure I can sustain it. I feel like I'm aging rapidly before my own eyes. And I don't know how to slow down without losing credibility."

Her voice cracked when she said it. That was the turning point.

What Amira didn't yet know is that the next level of leadership doesn't require more from you. It demands something different.

Presence. Perspective. Resilience. Discernment. All of that runs on one thing: energy.

Not adrenaline or overdrive. Not caffeine-powered chaos. **But sustainable, well-managed, deeply intentional energy.**

Energy always tells the truth. Even when your calendar says you're in control, your presence may say otherwise.

Why Energy Is a Strategic Asset

Time is finite. Energy, on the other hand, is renewable—if you know how to manage it.

Too many leaders treat energy as a background factor. They push themselves to the edge, then try to show up with presence, creativity, or compassion. But here's the truth: You can't offer what you don't have and great leadership is measured less by endurance and more by the ability to renew, recenter, and respond.

Research from The Energy Project and *Harvard Business Review* shows that when leaders manage energy across four dimensions—physical, emotional, mental, and spiritual—they perform better, avoid burnout, and increase engagement within their teams.

This is the energy shift: from output to presence, from overdrive to intention. The most effective leaders aren't the busiest. They're the most deliberate about where their energy goes.

Great leaders manage energy like elite swimmers, not by muscling through but by moving efficiently through resistance. Power isn't about thrashing harder. It's about aligning breath, focus, and flow.

MODEL: The Four Dimensions of Energy

Adapted from the work of Tony Schwartz and The Energy Project (HBR, 2007)

To manage your leadership energy intentionally, first understand the levers that drive it.

DIMENSION	WHAT IT FUELS	HOW TO STRENGTHEN IT
Physical	Stamina, vitality	Sleep, hydration, movement, nutrition
Emotional	Empathy, resilience	Boundaries, recovery, healthy connection, emotional processing
Mental	Focus, decision quality	Prioritization, mindfulness, time blocking
Spiritual	Purpose, values alignment	Reflection, service, connection to meaning

Confidence isn't just mental. It's energetic. When you're physically drained, emotionally flatlined, or mentally scattered, confidence evaporates—even if you know your content. Leaders often misread low energy as low ability. More often, it's fatigue speaking louder than skill.

► ELISE: Carrying Too Much

Elise was a VP of HR in a large healthcare system. Her reputation was impeccable. She was the leader everyone went to with problems, and she always made herself available. Her door was open, her phone buzzed late into the night, and she carried the weight of layoffs, conflicts, and personal crises like it was her responsibility to absorb them all.

At first, people loved her for it. But over time, Elise began to run down. She snapped at small things. She dreaded meetings. She felt oddly flat even when big wins came through. "I thought being a good leader meant being available all the time," she told me. "Now I feel like I don't have anything left to give."

I reminded her of something some leaders forget: at the end of the day, this is really just a job. It matters, yes. But it can't cost you everything. If you give it all away, the company will gladly take it.

What Elise was missing wasn't effort—it was recovery. She was spending all of her emotional energy outward, without putting anything back in.

We started small: a five-minute walk after heavy conversations. A ritual of writing down the hardest moment of the day, then closing the notebook. A "no calls" boundary after 8 p.m.

Within weeks, her team noticed a difference. Elise was still empathetic, but steadier. More present. She wasn't drained dry.

"I realized I don't have to carry everything to care deeply," she said. "I just have to stay whole."

Boundaries protect your energy. And energy is what makes empathy sustainable.

SPIRITUAL CUE: Return to Stillness

Spiritual teacher Ram Dass says, "The quieter you become, the more you can hear."

In many spiritual traditions, energy isn't just something you have. It's something you are. Your presence, clarity, and centeredness can't be faked. They emerge when your energy is aligned with your purpose.

Stillness, across sacred lineages, is not absence—it is activation. Jesus withdrew to quiet places. The Buddha sat under the Bodhi tree in silence for days. The Tao Te Ching teaches that "true stillness is the ruler of rest and motion."

Stillness wasn't avoidance. It was power.

Not weakness, but wisdom.

Leadership doesn't always mean doing. Sometimes, it means being in the *right relationship* with your own energy.

FIELD NOTE: Boundaries, Not Burnout

Millennials and Gen Z aren't lazy. They're listening to their nervous systems.

Younger leaders are beginning to push back against burnout culture. They unplug after hours. They set firmer boundaries. They value sustainability over martyrdom.

But boundaries are still a work in progress. Many protect their weekends for friendships, hobbies, or rest—even as they quietly battle the Sunday Scaries. They're not opting out of ambition. They're trying to write a different story about what success costs.

Many call it "protecting my peace." Not as an excuse to disengage, but as a way to create space for calm, presence, and recovery.

LinkedIn in 2023 reported that these leaders are redefining success by what's sustainable, not by what's more impressive.

It doesn't mean they care less. It means they want to stay in the game longer.

COACHING CUE: Be Meaningfully Engaged

Be careful not to confuse availability with presence. If you're always available, you're not fully present—you're just accessible.

True engagement means showing up with your full attention when it matters most. It's the leader who closes their laptop during one-on-ones. Who turns off Slack during strategic planning. Who says "I'm here" and actually means it.

Ask yourself: When was the last time you were truly present in a conversation—not just responsive but fully engaged? That's the shift from availability to presence.

The Busyness Trap: From Doing to Leading

One of the most consistent challenges I see in rising leaders is the inability—or unwillingness—to create white space in their schedules.

They stay stuck between doing and leading, carrying too much themselves instead of building the conditions for strategic leadership.

This transition is more than delegation. It's an identity shift: from being the reliable problem-solver to becoming the clear-eyed strategist who builds and empowers a strong team.

That shift isn't just strategic. It's energetic. You'll need physical energy to pace yourself, not power through. You'll need mental energy to see the system, not just the task. You'll need emotional energy to hold your team through uncertainty. And you'll need spiritual energy to remember why the shift matters. Leadership costs energy—just in different currency.

White space isn't wasted time. It's leadership time. It's where better ideas emerge, long-term decisions get made, and reflection becomes possible. Without it, leaders lose altitude.

Many clients fear that stepping back will be seen as disengagement or laziness. But in truth, the best executives protect white space. They make room for it in their calendar, they build buffer zones, and they use it to rise above the noise—and lead from the mountain, not the mine.

FIELD NOTE: Strategic Influence Versus Output

Leaders who prioritize white space often confront a deeper shift. Their value isn't tied to how much they do but to how they clarify priorities, shape direction, and move work forward through others.

Early in your career, output is the currency that gets you noticed. It's measurable, visible, and hard to argue with. You hit deadlines, deliver results and move fast.

But the higher you rise, the less your value is tied to output—and the more it depends on influence. Strategic clarity. Delegation. Decision-making under pressure.

The problem is that these forms of value are harder to see. And in the absence of visible contribution, many leaders default to over-functioning. They jump in. They overdeliver. They try to prove themselves all over again.

At senior levels, presence comes from doing what only you can do—and making sure others feel it.

That might include:

- The clarity you bring to ambiguity
- The conversations you shape
- The teams you grow and empower
- The cross-functional momentum you generate
- The culture you help define

These are harder to measure. But they're easier to feel. And they're what others will remember.

Ask yourself:

- Where am I still trying to prove my value through output?
- Where might I be confusing busyness with impact?
- What would it look like to lead through clarity, not activity?

This shift isn't a matter of letting go of performance. It's more about expanding how you define it—and how others experience it.

Leaders Who Prioritize White Space

Legendary investor Warren Buffett has long been known for protecting his calendar like a national treasure. He has spent as much as 80% of his day reading and thinking—a practice he credits with sharp decision-making. He once remarked, "The difference between successful people and really successful people is that really successful people say no to almost everything." To outsiders, his schedule might look empty. In truth, it's full of high-leverage thought.

Bill Gates, cofounder of Microsoft, became known for taking "think weeks"—solo retreats spent reading, reflecting, and anticipating big moves. Some of Microsoft's most innovative strategies emerged from those periods of solitude.

These stories are aspirational, but the principle isn't reserved for billionaires. In coaching, I recommend this practice to every leader I work with. The form it takes depends on your role and your season of leadership:

- For senior executives, it might mean a "sacred" hour of thinking time blocked by an assistant every afternoon, no exceptions.
- For mid-level leaders, it may be the first hour in the office before the day starts pulling at them.

- For others, it's one protected block toward the end of the day to clear their head and reset priorities before tomorrow.

It doesn't look the same in every function or rank, and it's harder if you don't run your own calendar. But in every case, the principle is the same: **white space isn't wasted time. It's leadership time.** And protecting it is one of the hardest, most worthwhile practices a leader can take on.

Suresh learned this the hard way.

► SURESH: Letting Go to Level Up

Suresh had built his career on being indispensable. A VP in logistics at a large national retailer, he knew the numbers, the routes, the systems, the people. He was the steady center of everything—and that was the problem.

His team respected him, but they relied on him for everything. Meetings stalled until he spoke. Problems piled up until he solved them. He wasn't just leading—he was bottlenecking.

"I like being needed," he admitted in one of our first sessions. "But if I'm not the one solving it, what's my value?"

That mindset had made him reliable. But it was now keeping him from being scalable.

Despite early coaching conversations about white space, he couldn't seem to create it. He filled his days with fire drills and approvals. He kept saying yes when he needed to say no.

Eventually, he gave his assistant full authority to protect one sacred time block each day—just 45 minutes. No drop-ins. No "quick questions." No meetings unless they were mission-critical. His assistant took to it with the zeal of a palace guard. Turns out, gatekeeping can be deeply satisfying when it's for a good cause.

For Suresh, it was awkward at first. He felt guilty, even worried his team would resent him for being less available. But he stuck with it. Over time, the new habit paid off. His team became more resourceful. They made faster decisions. They grew stronger and stopped depending on him.

And Suresh—for the first time in years—had space to think strategically, anticipate risks, and chart longer-term opportunities.

He became more visionary. He became scalable. And he finally stepped into the role his title had promised. Protecting that 45-minute block each day turned out to be the hardest—and most worthwhile—discipline of his leadership.

FIELD NOTE: The Cost of False Urgency

One of the biggest energy drains I see in high achievers is urgency addiction. Everything feels high stakes. Everything is "now."

But let's be honest: not everything is a fire. And not everything is yours to fix.

Remember Amira, the executive we met at the beginning of this chapter? Like many rising executives, she unintentionally trained her team to depend on her availability. She responded instantly. She jumped in to solve. She was the safety net.

She wasn't just burning out—she was becoming the bottleneck.

The shift came when she asked a better question: "Where can I step back and let others grow?"

Slowing down didn't diminish her leadership. It expanded her capacity.

AI can work 24/7 without burnout, but you can't. As automation accelerates, the value of human leadership won't be in keeping up. It will be in knowing when to slow down.

In the age of intelligent systems, wise energy management is no longer optional. Presence becomes your power source, not your performance metric.

You don't always need a full recharge. Sometimes, a micro reset is all it takes to recover presence.

TOOL: Micro Resets for Real Life

Here are some quick ways to refuel when time is short and pressure is high:

Physical: Step outside or walk a hallway for two minutes. Drop your shoulders. Stretch. Breathe through your nose for five deep cycles.

Mental: Close all tabs. (Yes, all 47 of them.) Name one thing you've already completed today. Write your next task on a Post-it and do only that.

Emotional: Text someone who lifts you up. Reframe: "I don't have to do this" → "I get to do this." Put your hand on your chest for ten seconds to reconnect with yourself.

Spiritual: Return to your why. Visualize who benefits from your leadership. Repeat a centering phrase like "be here now."

Small resets aren't minor. They're how presence rebuilds itself.

 READER-TO-LEADER: Managing Energy With Intention

Reflection:

- Which energy domain is most depleted for me right now—physical, emotional, mental, or spiritual?

- How does that depletion show up in my leadership presence?

- Am I addicted to urgency—or have I built a system for discernment?

- What habits signal I'm running on adrenaline instead of renewal?

Action:

- Audit your calendar: delegate, decline, or defer one task this week to create space for strategic thinking.

- Block 45 minutes of white space this week—treat it like a meeting with your CEO.

- Set one boundary that protects your recovery (e.g., no emails after 8 p.m., or a five-minute reset after hard conversations.)

INNER ALIGNMENT CUE: Return to Energy

Leadership begins with alignment—not just of priorities but of energy.

This week, ask yourself:

- Where is my energy clean and where is it entangled?

- Am I leading from clarity or from exhaustion?

- What would it look like to lead in alignment—letting energy carry me, instead of pushing through on effort alone?

Presence doesn't come from muscling through. It comes from managing your energy and your influence as though they matter—because they do.

> **REMEMBER THIS:** *Energy isn't just fuel—it's felt. When it's aligned, your presence carries more weight, more calm, and more credibility.*

WHEN THE WORK CHANGES

Leadership in the Age of AI

The shift is already underway.

Artificial intelligence isn't on its way. It has arrived—and it's rewriting work at a speed most people still underestimate. For many professionals, especially those in knowledge-based or mid-level leadership roles, this isn't just another wave of innovation. It's an existential turning point. Every role will change. Some will disappear. Some will expand. None will stay the same.

The question hanging in the air isn't *if* AI will change our work. It's *how fast*, and whether we'll adapt quickly enough to stay relevant.

That reality surfaced in a recent call with a prospective client—a thoughtful, capable, Millennial financial analyst working in the subscription media field. He's a bridge builder: someone who connects data and meaning, who helps people see what the numbers are trying to say.

His organization's founders are obsessed with AI. So is the senior team. Four months earlier, they brought in a team of ten AI specialists who are already implementing sweeping changes—including a company-specific version of ChatGPT designed to know everything about the enterprise and able to perform a wide array of analysis. They see it all as opportunity, optimization, inevitability—and they're not wrong. But they've moved so quickly that something human is being lost in the process.

He said something I can't forget: "They're so enamored with what AI can do, they've forgotten we're still here."

He recently overheard a conversation between a colleague who compiles the advance packet for the board of directors—a time-intensive, highly tailored document for senior decision-makers—and their shared manager. The manager casually asked, "Isn't there an AI program that could do this for us?" His colleague replied, "Yes, there probably is, but then what would I do?" They both laughed nervously.

That moment landed hard. Not because it was cruel but because it was so casual. The implication was clear: *your function might be next.* And no one was talking about it directly.

He wasn't asking to stop the future. He was asking to be part of it.

Transformation at Warp Speed

AI is a lightning rod, but it's not the only disruption reshaping work. Every leader today stands in the crossfire of simultaneous shifts—economic, cultural, generational, and technological. AI hasn't arrived as a spark; it's an accelerant poured on an already burning platform.

This is not incremental change. It's exponential. The pace of transformation is now outpacing human adaptation. What once took a decade now happens in a quarter. And in that widening gap between what's technically possible and what people can emotionally process, leadership either steps up—or culture fractures.

When the ground moves this fast, people don't just need direction. They need orientation—an internal compass to know where they stand, how they contribute, and what still holds true.

This is why presence matters more now than ever. In the previous chapter, we explored how leaders manage energy across physical, mental, emotional, and spiritual dimensions. Now, we move from internal sustainability to external disruption. Because when the work changes rapidly, **leaders become the stability.** Not by pushing harder, but by anchoring deeper.

Most senior leaders don't mean to dismiss people when they embrace innovation. But in their urgency to move forward, they often skip the very work that makes change stick: *Translation. Inclusion. Reassurance. Listening.*

AI disruption isn't just operational. It's psychological. It changes how people understand their value. It triggers survival fear. It surfaces old insecurities: Am I replaceable? Is my judgment still relevant? Do they even need me?

This is why grounded, transparent, attuned leadership isn't optional anymore. It's the differentiator between adoption that energizes and adoption that alienates.

📌 MODEL: The AI Disruption Equation

Tech Acceleration + Identity Ambiguity → Presence Crisis

When roles shift faster than leaders speak to the human experience of that shift, fragmentation sets in:

- High performers stop speaking up.
- Mid-level leaders defer or disconnect.
- Cultures turn anxious or performative

All this happens not because people are fragile. It's because they feel unseen.

This equation comes to life when organizations move faster

than they communicate. **Tech Acceleration** isn't just the introduction of new tools. It's the pace of implementation that outstrips people's ability to mentally recalibrate their value. **Identity Ambiguity** emerges when people can't clearly answer, "What's still mine to do?" The result is a **Presence Crisis**—people remain visible but disengage energetically. Their bodies are in the room, yet their insight and confidence have left.

The pattern is remarkably consistent across industries. In financial services, analysts stop volunteering insights. In health care, mid-level administrators become procedural rather than proactive. In tech companies, project managers defer to algorithmic recommendations, even when their human judgment would add crucial nuance.

What makes this crisis particularly insidious is its subtlety. Unlike layoffs or restructurings, this fragmentation happens without drama. Performance reviews still look fine, yet the sparks that fuel innovation—the "what if" conversations, the cross-silo connections, the intuitive catches—start to vanish.

Here's how this looked in a recent client situation.

When AI Silences the Floor

One client—a Director in a global, tech-adjacent retail organization—shared a story that stopped me cold.

Their senior leadership team had introduced a customized chatbot to handle onboarding, write meeting summaries, and draft internal communications. The technology worked. The launch appeared smooth. But within three weeks, engagement in team meetings dropped sharply. People started turning cameras off. Questions dried up.

Eventually, a junior team member named it: "It feels like there's no point in speaking up anymore. The system already wrote the answers."

The technology didn't hurt trust. The silence did.

The rollout removed friction, but it also removed invitation. No one clarified what leadership still expected from humans.

If you don't name what's still wanted, people will assume they're not needed.

COACHING CUE: Change Without Inclusion Feels Like Threat

You cannot coach someone through transformation without first acknowledging that it feels threatening.

That doesn't mean indulging fear. It means naming it, witnessing it, and giving it somewhere to go.

Say what's real:

- "Most roles are changing. That's true."
- "AI will likely replace certain tasks. That's also true."
- "We intend to grow our people into the future—not erase them."

People don't need rehearsed optimism. They need clarity. And they need to know their leaders aren't outsourcing empathy to the next app rollout.

What AI Can't Replace

AI will surpass human capability in speed, scale, and optimization. What it cannot replicate—at least for now—are the capacities that hold organizations together:

HUMAN CAPACITY	AI COUNTERPART	WHERE THE LINE STILL HOLDS—FOR NOW
Contextual judgment	Data pattern matching	Still struggles with nuance in messy, emotional, or politically charged settings
Relational presence	Scripted output	Can simulate empathy but cannot feel or attune in real time
Strategic pausing	Continuous response	Has no sense of timing or when silence carries more weight than words
Coaching and listening	Prompt response	Can mirror questions but not perceive energy, body language, or trust signals
Moral/ethical discernment	Programmed constraint	Executes boundaries, yet lacks internal conscience and emotional consequence

These edges are narrowing quickly. The question isn't whether AI will learn to mimic these behaviors—it's whether it will ever mean them.

For now, depth of awareness, genuine empathy, and ethical courage remain human work. As AI grows more capable, those traits won't become less important; they'll become the final measure of trust.

Here's the paradox of our time: As machines master the predictable, humans inherit the unpredictable. The ability to stay steady in uncertainty is becoming a defining leadership skill.

AI can already answer "how" and "what." For now, it still depends on humans to answer "why it matters" and to hold the meaning behind the data.

The mechanical parts of work will continue to evolve. The human parts—discernment, empathy, and presence—will keep their value for as long as trust and emotion shape decisions.

FIELD NOTE: The Hidden Trauma of Disruption

As technology accelerates, identity doesn't always keep pace. The human system wobbles before it recalibrates.

AI doesn't just change workflows; it shakes identity. When people feel their expertise is suddenly obsolete, the loss runs deeper than a task list. It feels like: Who am I here? Do I still matter?

That sense of erasure can be deeply destabilizing. For some, it shows up as a disorientation or withdrawal. For others, especially when disruption is repeated or high-stakes, it can resemble chronic stress—hypervigilance, anxiety, or the sense of being unsafe in a place that once felt stable.

Leaders don't need to diagnose these reactions, but they do need to recognize that the stress is real, and the impact is deep. If disruption is treated as a purely operational challenge, the human cost gets ignored. And what goes unacknowledged doesn't disappear. It drives disengagement underground, where it erodes trust and engagement from within.

What helps isn't spin or platitudes. It's presence. Name the loss. Listen without judgment. Make space for people to voice what feels endangered. In moments of disruption, acknowledgment is not weakness. It's the first step in helping people find their footing again.

 TOOL: Leading Through Tech Disruption

Here's how to lead with presence through tech disruption.

Acknowledge: Name the change clearly and calmly. Avoid euphemisms. People can handle truth better than silence.

Translate: Help your team understand what's shifting and why. Context reduces anxiety and speeds up alignment.

Include: Invite questions and surface concerns. Ask what feels uncertain or at risk, and listen fully before responding.

Elevate: Spotlight the distinctly human contributions that technology can't yet replicate—collaboration, judgment, empathy.

Coach: Model steadiness. You don't need perfect answers, but you do need visible presence. Say: "We're going to walk this forward, together."

Leaders who combine technological fluency with emotional presence will define how well their organizations adapt—and how much trust survives the change.

► BRIANNA: Elevating Humans While Embracing AI

Brianna led product operations at a fast-growing logistics platform. When her company announced its AI integration strategy, she knew her team would be directly affected. Rather than waiting for corporate scripts, she pulled her team into the process early.

She created a whiteboard with two columns: **Tasks AI Could Likely Take** and **Human Value We Still Need.** Then she invited the team to fill them in together.

At first, there were hesitant glances—no one wanted to name what might disappear. But as the conversation unfolded, something shifted. They began to see their work differently. The focus moved from tasks to value and from fear to ownership.

What emerged was more than a list—it was a reframing. The team began to see themselves not just as executors of work but as interpreters of complexity, connectors of people, and stewards of meaning.

One of her engineers said, "I'm not afraid of AI anymore. I'm afraid of being invisible. But now I see where I still shine."

Brianna's approach wasn't flashy. It was precise, inclusive, and deeply human. She didn't just manage the transition—she dignified it.

Her leadership worked because she addressed every part of

the **AI Disruption Equation.** First, she slowed **Tech Acceleration** by giving her team time to process and participate. She reduced **Identity Ambiguity** through shared language and visible contribution in the whiteboard exercise. And ultimately, she prevented a **Presence Crisis** by making people visible in the solution, not casualties of it.

This is what it looks like to lead through transformation without losing your people—or yourself.

The Next Frontier: What Leaders Will Face

AI is moving rapidly from task automation to decision orchestration. Very soon—likely within the span of this book's shelf life—leaders won't just manage people and projects. They'll be managing systems that think alongside human colleagues in real time.

That shift raises complex questions: How do you hold accountability when the "teammate" is an algorithm? How do you integrate ethics and human oversight into workflows designed for speed? How do you preserve discernment when technology tempts you to outsource it?

These questions aren't theoretical anymore. They are showing up in hiring decisions, budget reviews, and customer interactions. This is why ethical discernment and sense-making are no longer optional leadership skills. Tools can optimize, but humans contextualize. And the leaders who hold that line will be the ones others trust to set the course.

As AI expands its reach, leadership will depend less on knowing answers and more on framing the right questions. The next era of influence will belong to those who combine technical fluency with emotional and ethical depth.

TOOL: Future-Proofing Your Leadership

As AI continues to reshapes how work gets done, your edge won't be what you **can** do. It will be what only you **should** do.

These are the skills and signals that future-proof your leadership:

- Synthesis and sense-making. Connecting insights across silos in real time, identifying patterns others miss.

- Emotional intelligence. Reading the room, adjusting tone, building trust through calm and clarity.

- Coaching and people development. Growing capability and confidence in others, not just driving output.

- Ethical discernment. Weighing impact, integrity, and consequences as part of every decision.

- Energetic presence. Setting tone, pace, and emotional safety through how you show up.

Let AI do what scales. Protect and refine what *grounds*.

The tools will evolve. The differentiator will remain your ability to connect meaning, ethics, and momentum in real time.

Beyond Efficiency: The Hidden Costs of AI

As organizations scale their AI strategies, a deeper truth is surfacing: efficiency has a cost. Large systems consume vast energy and water resources. They reshape how we think about data privacy, authorship, and autonomy. They even alter how teams experience time—speeding the clock for some, slowing it for others.

Leaders who ignore these realities risk eroding trust. The future will reward those who **balance technological adoption with human and environmental sustainability.** When you name the tradeoffs and keep well-being visible in the conversation, you remind your people that progress doesn't have to mean depletion.

Efficiency and sustainability are part of the external challenge. But presence—the way you show up inside that challenge—is what people will remember most.

SPIRITUAL CUE: Technology Is Not the Enemy. Disconnection Is.

In the Tao Te Ching, Lao Tzu teaches that true power lies not in force but in alignment with the natural flow. Applied to leadership, that means staying rooted as systems shift—responding without resistance and advancing without losing center.

AI is not the storm. Fear is what unsettles people. And your calm presence is the shelter.

This is the moment to lead with clarity—not panic, not performance. Stay alert to what people aren't saying. Stay generous with your attention. Stay human.

In a world of instant responses, taking time to truly listen becomes radical. When AI can generate reports in seconds, the leader who pauses long enough to hear someone's concern creates irreplaceable trust. Your attention becomes the gift that says, "You matter beyond your output."

Technology may shape the tools. But you still shape the tone, the trust, and the future.

The Leadership Frontier

Looking ahead, leaders will face questions once reserved for policymakers and scientists:

- How do we regulate what we create?
- How do we reinvent ourselves fast enough to stay relevant?
- How do we build cultures of learning instead of cultures of fear?

These are not abstract issues. They're arriving at every level of leadership. Your steadiness, transparency, and willingness to lead through ambiguity will determine how your teams move through them. The tools will continue to evolve, but leadership will remain a human act—grounded in awareness, accountability, and connection.

Presence is no longer a soft skill. It's strategic infrastructure for the future of work.

COACHING IMPERATIVE: AI Awareness Is Now a Core Leadership Skill

Leaders who fail to understand AI's capabilities and limits won't just fall behind—they'll become unemployable.

Every role that influences people, money, or information will soon require working fluency with AI systems. You don't need to be a coder, but you do need to know what these tools can do, where they can fail, and how they reshape trust.

Ignorance is no longer harmless; it's a liability. Mastering AI awareness is now part of your professional duty to stay relevant to lead responsibly.

READER-TO-LEADER: Staying Human in a Time of Machines

Reflect:

- Where am I quietly afraid of being replaced?
- What part of my value feels harder to measure in an AI-driven world?
- What new responsibilities—ethical, environmental, cultural—might I need to steward as AI accelerates?
- How can I prepare myself and my team to adapt with clarity instead of fear?

Act:

- Write one sentence that captures the value you bring that no AI could authentically replicate—yet.

- Ask a peer or mentor to reflect back what they rely on you for.

- Run your own version of Brianna's whiteboard exercise. Make two columns—Tasks Tech Can Take and Human Value We Still Bring. Fill them in together with your team.

- Bring the human value you named into one conversation this week—on purpose.

- Choose one emerging frontier (AI agents, ethics, sustainability, reskilling) and take one small step: read, ask, or act.

REMEMBER THIS: *The technology will keep changing. Your relevance depends on claiming the leadership only humans can still bring—presence, discernment, and the courage to stay awake as the world transforms.*

OWNING THE ROOM

Gravitas You Can Grow

Gravitas is often mistaken for charisma—the magnetic quality you're either born with or cultivate. But gravitas is something deeper; it is the weight of presence that makes people listen. And it's something every leader can build. I learned that lesson in a most unexpected way.

I was 30 years old, walking across a silent city square in Budapest, Hungary, to meet the president of the United States.

I didn't plan to. I didn't even think it was possible. But then it happened—and what I learned about presence in one brief encounter has stayed with me ever since.

That day in December 1994, I was working on the seventh floor of the Hungarian Foreign Trade Bank. I'd been placed there through the MBA Enterprise Corps, a public-private initiative supporting economic development in post-communist Europe, and I was the first Westerner the bank had ever hired.

It was the day of the historic Budapest Memorandum on Security Assurances—a diplomatic gathering of the United

States, the United Kingdom, Ukraine, and Russia that marked a turning point in post-Cold War security.

While world leaders met across town, the mayor of Budapest asked residents to stay home to keep the streets clear. But I had a deal deadline, and a few colleagues and I were at our desks, where our office windows overlooked St. Stephen's Basilica in the heart of the city.

As I worked, a colleague ran toward me, wide-eyed.

"Your president! Your president! He's at the Basilica—come look!"

I rushed to the window, and in the square was a black SUV motorcade with American flags and Bill Clinton inside one car.

My colleagues insisted I go down and try to meet him. I grabbed my coat and my passport (just in case) and headed out. The square was eerily quiet. I joined a tiny group of curious locals standing near a makeshift security perimeter, guarded by the US Secret Service. It was clear this wasn't a scheduled stop. Clinton had likely gone off-script, as he often did.

Moments later, he emerged from the church, his arm around the shoulders of a young, slightly stunned priest. As the president approached the waiting motorcade, we started waving—and to our shock (and maybe the Secret Service's horror), he turned and walked toward us.

I saw my chance.

"Mr. President—I'm Kathryn Lowell, and I'm from Arkansas!"

He stopped, surprised.

"Well, I'll be! What? What are you doing here?"

I explained quickly—my work, the bank, my Arkansas roots. I pointed up to the seventh floor, where my colleagues were waving like crazy. He laughed, and that's when it happened.

Everything else fell away.

In that moment, it felt like there was no motorcade, no security, no others—just two people in a real conversation. He looked directly at me. He listened. He asked thoughtful questions. And he made me feel fully seen.

Even though I had grown up in Arkansas, I'd never met him. But now, here we were, two Arkansans unexpectedly meeting in far-off Budapest. He asked about my hometown, and of course, he knew it. I was nervous, but his warmth and focus put me at ease instantly.

After a minute or two—maybe more—I thanked him and stepped back so he could move on. He walked to the car, waving once more.

And then, as the motorcade began to roll away, the window slid down.

"Hey, Kathryn, where are your parents from? What brought them to Arkansas?"

I replied quickly. One more moment. One more layer of connection. And then he was gone.

That brief encounter taught me something I've never forgotten: **presence isn't about power. It's about focus.** It's the rare individual, even if it's the most powerful man in the world, who has the ability to make the stranger in front of them feel like the only other person in the room.

That experience taught me to recognize presence in others and to understand how I wanted to embody it myself. But what makes presence land in leadership? And how do you build it if it doesn't come naturally?

Presence Is Not Volume. It's Voltage

Some people command attention the moment they enter a room. That doesn't mean they're the most powerful voice in it.

Gravitas is the unmistakable signal that you're someone to listen to. And it can be cultivated.

And for rising leaders, it's often the missing ingredient that determines whether others see you as leadership-ready.

Before we dive into building gravitas, let's name something that's often left vague—and why that matters.

FRAMEWORK: The Presence Landscape

Presence. Gravitas. Charisma. Executive presence.

These terms get used constantly in leadership conversations, yet most people can't define them clearly. Worse, they're often conflated. One leader's "gravitas" is another's "charisma." And when someone says, "You need more executive presence," it often lands like a vague, unhelpful judgment.

In my coaching practice, I break them down like this:

TERM	WHAT IT REALLY MEANS
PRESENCE	The energetic impact of your attention. Are you grounded and attuned, here? People feel it before you say a word.
GRAVITAS	The weight of your presence—the sense that you have something worth listening to. It shows up as clarity, composure, and confidence under pressure.
CHARISMA	The magnetic pull of your energy—a warmth, expressiveness, or emotional spark that draws people in. Charisma can amplify presence, but it's not required for influence. (One caveat: when charm isn't grounded in substance, it can feel hollow, even manipulative.)
EXECUTIVE PRESENCE	The combination of visual, verbal, and energetic signals that communicate credibility and leadership readiness—especially in senior-level environments.

I support leaders as they build all four of these dimensions. But it starts with clarity. You can't amplify something you haven't defined. When they see these terms defined, most leaders breathe a sigh of relief. What once felt like a dead end of feedback becomes a clear path forward. They can see which lever they need to pull— grounding their presence, strengthening gravitas, dialing up charisma, or signaling executive readiness. Once the fog lifts, they finally have somewhere to focus their effort. And that clarity alone can be a game changer.

► LEO: When Confidence Doesn't Land

Leo was a Senior Director of Product Innovation, responsible for driving strategy in a fast-moving, highly visible part of the business. He had good relationships, a strong track record, and sharp instincts. But in high-stakes meetings, something didn't land.

He didn't speak often, but when he did, he rushed his words. His sentences trailed off. He sometimes looked away mid-thought or backtracked with disclaimers. One executive commented, "He's clearly smart, but I feel like he's running from his own point."

In the room, Leo looked like he was trying to disappear into his slouched posture and downward gaze; he seemed to be physically retreating in his chair. His presence didn't match his seniority or his potential.

And the perception became self-fulfilling. His ideas were overlooked. He wasn't tapped for stretch assignments. Others in the room assumed he didn't want more, when, in fact, he did.

In our coaching, we didn't work on making Leo louder. We worked on making him **land**. Anchoring his posture. Breathing before he spoke. Choosing declarative statements over qualifiers. Holding eye contact comfortably. The goal was simple: let his inside match his outside and be the same person in the room that he was in his head.

Once he began aligning his delivery with the substance he already had, the shift was immediate. People started listening longer. He was asked to co-lead a new cross-functional initiative. One of his peers even said, "You walk into the room differently now. Like someone we're supposed to listen to."

Leo didn't become someone else. He simply started showing up fully as himself—without all the habits that had been getting in his way. The work was always about clearing out what was blocking who he already was.

You might recognize here echoes of the **Tentative Striver** profile from Chapter 3. But this time, we're moving from confidence into full presence and exploring what happens when strength isn't expressed in a way others can feel.

► JD: Too Much Airtime

JD was a VP in a large organization's technical operations group. He had sharp insight, natural charisma, and was widely admired. His technical knowledge was unmatched, and his presence lit up any room. He was the kind of leader people naturally followed.

But as he stepped into more senior forums, his gravitas wasn't landing the way it needed to.

Through the 360-feedback interview process, we uncovered a pattern: he talked too much. One senior leader quipped, "If I ask you to show me your watch, you don't have to tell me how it was built!" His deep knowledge and enthusiasm often led him to overexplain or go into granular detail. It began to wear on peers, who—while fans of JD—were tired of how much airtime he used. It also occasionally overwhelmed senior leaders and unintentionally diminished his direct reports.

Instead of creating space for others to grow, he inadvertently took the stage himself. Instead of trusting his team to deliver a message, he'd jump in to clarify or add color—sometimes undercutting them in the process.

Our work focused on recalibrating his presence: learning to pause, reading the room, and trusting that silence doesn't mean disengagement but respect.

JD practiced yielding the floor and began using fewer, more

potent words. He started noticing the moments when he could step back to let others contribute, especially his direct reports. By creating more space, he gave his team opportunities to grow and demonstrate their strengths.

Within two months, the shift was palpable. When the company expanded his remit and recognized the impact of his leadership, they created a new Senior Vice President role specifically for him—not just for what he knew, but for how he showed up.

JD mirrored the other end of the spectrum—what Chapter 3 called the **Presentation-Perfect Performer.** His confidence was real, but it wasn't calibrated for the room. Presence is as much about what you withhold as what you express.

► MEERA: When Calm Gets Misread

Meera was a Senior Manager in enterprise systems. Originally from India, she had been working in the U.S. for over a decade. She was known for her reliability, strong technical judgment, and calm demeanor. Her team respected her, and her results were solid. But when it came to visibility with senior leaders, she kept getting passed over.

Her peers described her as "quiet but competent," and one leader commented that, "She doesn't really light up the room or take control in meetings."

When we reviewed video recordings of meetings, it became clear: Meera rarely spoke unless asked. When she did, her voice softened, her sentences were short, and her gaze dropped quickly. In pressure situations, her calmness veered toward detachment.

What made her effective one-on-one wasn't translating in larger rooms. And it wasn't just about her speaking volume. It was about energetic clarity, the ability to project steady leadership in moments of uncertainty.

We worked on projecting steadiness without disappearing:

holding eye contact longer, infusing her calm tone with clarity and conviction, rehearsing what it sounded like to speak not just as a subject-matter expert but as a leader carrying the room forward.

The biggest shift? Her energy. She began practicing something we called "centered authority"—that subtle but powerful signal that says, "I've got you." Not louder. Not flashier. Just more present.

Within a quarter, Meera was asked to co-lead a strategic transformation initiative. And her team? They began reflecting the very centered energy she had learned to transmit.

FIELD NOTE: Digital Gravitas—Owning the Zoom Room

Gravitas isn't just for conference rooms. It translates directly into virtual spaces. The stakes can feel higher on Zoom, where your face *is* your presence.

Virtual settings amplify presence gaps. But they also magnify even small shifts.

Here are the habits I coach most often to help clients transmit credibility on-screen:

- Use a high-quality camera and good lighting that illuminates your entire face.
- Choose a clean, neutral background.
- Turn your camera on, visibility equals credibility.
- Look at the camera when speaking (simulate eye contact).
- Frame your face and shoulders well.
- Show that you're present: nod, react, engage.
- Speak with slightly more vocal energy than feels natural.
- Model virtual etiquette: no multitasking, full presence.

Even small adjustments elevate your presence. According to

facial communication expert Paul Ekman, people assess trust-worthiness, confidence, and credibility in milliseconds—especially when your face is their only visual cue.

Younger leaders are often more fluent in camera dynamics, thanks to platforms like Snapchat and TikTok, where eye contact, gesture, and tone are embedded in the native language of digital expression.

What I often remind leaders is this: you don't need to perform for the camera, but you do need to *transmit through it*. That means treating the lens as one more room you can learn to own. The same centered presence that steadies a boardroom can travel down a webcam—if you're intentional.

COACHING INSIGHT: When Gravitas Comes at a Cost

For many leaders—especially women, BIPOC and LGBTQ+ professionals, and others whose identities fall outside dominant leadership norms—showing up with presence isn't just a skill. It's a risk.

They often face double binds—situations where any choice carries a penalty. These conflicting expectations involve consequences, no matter how they show up. For example, a woman who speaks with conviction may be called aggressive. If she softens her tone, she risks being dismissed as uncertain.

Their reality often includes:

- Feeling pressure to overprepare, over function, and outperform just to be seen as credible.

- Managing how passion is perceived. Too much intensity can be read as threatening; too little can be read as disengaged.

- Being hyperaware of stereotypes, biases, and the need to represent more than just themselves.

This additional labor isn't theoretical. It's emotional, mental, and energetic—and it's often invisible to those who haven't lived it.

One young professional I spoke with—a gay man early in his corporate career—shared that his well-meaning boss often overemphasized his identity in awkward ways. The manager meant well, but the greater focus felt performative. As a result, the employee found himself shrinking—not because he felt unsafe but because he was managing the discomfort of someone else's learning curve. That wasn't his job, but he felt the weight of it anyway. Inclusion isn't about over accommodating or underreacting. It's about attunement.

In coaching, I hold space for this complexity. I validate the reality of the minefields, without making them the whole story.

True support means helping leaders:

- Honor the extra emotional load they are carrying.

- Build tools to recover, recenter, and protect their energy.

- Claim agency—choosing where and how they want to be seen, rather than constantly reacting to external perceptions.

- Cultivate support systems that recognize, replenish, and respect their leadership journey.

Presence has a price. But it can also become a profound source of self-mastery and influence—when it's carried with intention, not just endurance.

COACHING CUE: Conscious Presence in Double Binds

If you're navigating the added complexity of double binds, stereotypes, or bias, conscious presence becomes more than a leadership skill. It's an act of agency.

- Recognize the double binds without internalizing them.

- Choose when and how to step forward—strategically, not reflexively.

- Build circles of support inside and outside your organization where you can be fully seen and restored.

• Reframe visibility as agency: "I choose how I am seen and why."

Gravitas isn't about erasing who you are. It's about owning your space with wisdom, agency, and strategic clarity

✕ TOOL: The Gravitas Builders

Gravitas isn't about being the most extroverted person in the room. It's about showing up with clarity, calm, and conviction under pressure. Here are five powerful ways to cultivate gravitas[3]:

1. **Use the strategic pause:** Stop rushing. Slow your speech. Let silence work for you.

2. **Own your seat:** Sit fully upright, lean in slightly, plant your feet. You belong here. Research from **Amy Cuddy** and others shows that posture and nonverbal confidence impact not just how others see us, but how we experience ourselves.

3. **Decide what you believe:** Before you speak, clarify your stance. Don't dilute the strength of your message with caveats.

4. **Control your hands:** No fidgeting, tapping, or too much gesturing. Let stillness underscore your confidence.

5. **Be the calm in the room:** Especially in moments of tension. That's when people look to the leader.

When you master these fundamentals, people will start listening before you even speak.

---

3 For additional tools on posture, visual presence, and polish, including attire, grooming, and etiquette for high-stakes moments, as well as notes on the power of first impressions, see Appendixes I and II.

FIELD NOTE: Gravitas Across Cultures

Gravitas is often assessed through a Western, extrovert-leaning lens, where confidence is equated with assertiveness, projection, and decisiveness. But leadership presence looks different across cultures.

In many East Asian and South Asian contexts, humility, deference, and indirect speech are associated with wisdom and maturity. In African, Latin American, and Indigenous cultures, relational energy—not just articulation—carries authority. What feels powerful in one context may feel passive or aggressive in another.

For global or bicultural leaders, this creates tension:

- How do I speak with strength in a way that still feels like me?

- How do I read the room without losing my roots?

- How do I adapt without masking?

COACHING CUE:

Don't ask: How do I conform?

Ask: What impact do I want to have and how can I translate my strength into this room's language, without abandoning my own?

Try this:

- Choose one value you want to embody (e.g., wisdom, steadiness, respect).

- Identify how that value is typically expressed in your home culture.

- Now ask: What is the clearest way I can signal that same value here—using visible behaviors this audience will read?

You're not becoming someone else. You're bridging. That's a leadership act.

SPIRITUAL CUE: Embodied Stillness

In moments of pressure, great leaders don't fill the room with noise. They anchor it with presence.

This echoes the Taoist concept of *wu wei*—effortless action that comes from alignment with one's true nature. As Lao Tzu wrote, "Nature does not hurry, yet everything is accomplished." In leadership, your centered presence creates a container for others to find their own clarity.

Buddha taught that calm is not indifference, but the highest form of strength. In the Gospels, Jesus calmed the storm with a few words.

Gravitas doesn't come from pushing. It comes from centered clarity.

Ask: *Can I settle myself enough to settle the room?*

BREATH PRACTICE: The Four-Point Frequency Reset

This practice is adapted from contemplative traditions and performance coaching. Use it before a high-stakes meeting—or as your centering ritual before clicking "Join."

1. **Inhale deeply (four counts):** Draw breath through your spine. Fill your lungs.

2. **Hold (four counts):** Set your intention: *I am calm, I am focused, I am generous, I am clear.*

3. **Exhale (four counts):** Let go of tension. Release fear, distraction, ego.

4. **Stillness (four counts):** Be present in the pause. Feel your center. Arrive.

As Eckhart Tolle teaches, true power lives in the now. This practice brings you there.

As we explored in Chapter 4, perception starts before you

speak. It's shaped by tone, timing, posture, presence, and what others expect from someone in your role.

So how do you know what others are perceiving? The Gravitas Spectrum helps decode where your presence might be landing and how to recalibrate.

MODEL: The Gravitas Spectrum

Gravitas shows up on a spectrum. At one end, it can feel under-powered—muted, hesitant, or unclear. At the other, it tips into overbearing by dominating the room, oversharing, or pushing too hard. Use this model to find where you naturally land and consider how to recalibrate.

Here's what the spectrum looks like in practice:

UNDERPOWERED	BALANCED	OVERBEARING
Tentative speech; excessive qualifiers	Clear, steady tone and message	Monopolizing conversation; overexplaining
Shrinking posture; energetically withdrawn	Grounded posture and calm presence	Overly assertive stance; performative energy
Avoids eye contact	Intentional, steady eye contact	Intense or unrelenting gaze
Disappears in crisis; delays decisions	Brings calm authority and timely action	Escalates tension; acts impulsively
Muddled or unclear messaging	Concise, declarative communication	Dominates with detail; rigid delivery
Deflects credit; hesitant to take space	Confident humility; visible ownership	Spotlight-seeking; ego-driven presence

Most of us have a default pattern that has us shrinking to stay safe or inflating to feel seen. The goal isn't to be perfect. It's to notice your pattern so you can choose differently when it matters most.

If the Gravitas Spectrum shows you where you stand, this next ritual gives you a way to practice moving upward—one meeting at a time.

TOOL: Three-Part Meeting Ritual

My favorite leadership ritual for learning how to own the room is to treat every meeting as not one but as three meetings: 1) the pre-meeting, 2) the main meeting, and 3) the post-meeting.

1. The pre-meeting: This is *your* meeting.

Passing through the doorframe is your reset. Whatever happened before—the last meeting, the difficult conversation, the pile of unread emails—let it all go as you enter. Settle your energy and step into presence. Arrive just a little early, even a minute or two, to give yourself this space.

As you walk in, notice: people will typically look up. Even the ones on their phone or computer will glance up for a second. Catch those eyes. Smile. Greet. Don't rush to find your seat— use that moment to engage. Introduce yourself to someone new. Connect two people who don't know each other. Sit beside someone you wouldn't normally sit next to. Spark a conversation.

In these moments, you are hosting, even if you're not running the meeting. And *that's* leadership. You're seen as open, confident, approachable, relaxed. And you are quietly claiming authority—the kind of power that earns trust before the agenda even begins.

I often say: "The meeting may not be yours. But the pre-meeting definitely is."

2. The main meeting: Anchor the room.

Once the meeting begins, your presence matters as much as your words. Sit upright but at ease—alert without stiffness. Let your eyes and expressions show you're tracking the discussion. People don't just hear you: they're reading you.

When you speak, don't rush. Pace yourself and make your points crisp and intentional. And resist the urge to dominate. At worst, meetings can feel like captivity—and if you're taking all the oxygen, you've become the jailer.

Put devices away. Glancing at emails or texts signals disinterest, and if someone is making an important point, they'll remember the moment you looked away.

If you're running the meeting, honor the clock. Keep discussions moving when they drift. What carries weight here is not showmanship. It's steadiness and intentional participation.

3. The post-meeting: Make it personal.

When the meeting ends, most people pack up fast—heads down, rushing to the next thing. That's your opportunity to stand out. This is where influence compounds.

Start with appreciation. Thank the facilitator with a specific comment. Call out a colleague's insight or effort. Notice who spoke up with courage and give them a quiet word of recognition. These gestures travel farther than you think.

And then, don't sprint for the door. Choose one person to walk and talk with on the way out. It can be a peer, a junior teammate, or someone you don't know well. Those two minutes of casual connection often carry more weight than the entire agenda.

Think of it as the "parking-lot MBA." The little conversations on the way out of the room often teach you more—and build more trust—than the slides ever did.

The post-meeting is where relationships deepen. Skip it, and you've left influence on the table.

READER-TO-LEADER: Leading the Room with Gravitas

Reflect:

- In high-stakes settings, where do you tend to land on the Gravitas Spectrum—underpowered, balanced, or overbearing?

- How do race, gender, culture, or generational identity shape the expectations you face around presence?

- When do you rely on performance instead of presence? What would it look like to let pause, silence or steadiness do the work instead?

- How do you want others to feel when you speak—and how closely does your current presence match that intention?

Act:

- Practice the Three-Part Meeting Ritual this week: ground before, anchor during, and connect after.

- Ask for feedback: What's it like to be in a room when I'm speaking? When I'm listening?

- Choose one of the Gravitas Builders—like tone, stance, or breath—listed earlier in this chapter, and intentionally experiment with it in a visible setting.

> **REMEMBER THIS:** *Gravitas isn't inherited. It's practiced. Chosen. Embodied. Leadership presence isn't about perfection. It's about the energy, alignment, and credibility you carry, without speaking a word. In the end, it's not just what you say. It's what you transmit.*

FROM REACTION TO RESPONSE

Why Pause Is Power

It's one thing to walk into a room with gravitas. It's another to hold that presence when pressure spikes.

In leadership, pressure isn't the exception. It's the environment. Meetings where voices rise. Deadlines that close in. Crises hit without warning. The higher you go, the more eyes watch how you respond in the moment.

In those moments, your prepared words matter—but so do the signals that slip out in the pauses: the sigh, the glance, the tone that sharpens before you catch it. Reaction is fast—sometimes faster than your common sense. Those signals shape how much people trust you when stakes are high.

Camille learned this the hard way.

► CAMILLE: When Reactions Override Intent

Camille led the regulatory function for a large consumer goods company. A brilliant legal mind, she had earned her VP title through relentless hard work, fierce intelligence, and an unwavering sense of duty to the business. Her team respected her competence and knew she had their backs.

But during a round of confidential interviews as part of her coaching engagement, a troubling theme emerged: Camille's team didn't feel safe bringing her bad news. Several direct reports described how her face would contort, her body would stiffen, or she'd sigh heavily when they brought her challenges.

"You could just feel her disappointment," one person said. "She doesn't yell. But you can feel it. And it makes me not want to tell her the truth."

This **emotional leakage**—completely unintended—created a perception problem. Camille genuinely cared about her people. She routinely celebrated their wins, hosted small appreciation events (often on her own dime), and was known for handwritten thank-you notes. But when things went wrong, her body language carried a message she didn't intend.

Camille and I worked closely on emotional regulation—not to suppress her reactions but to notice them in real time. She began tuning into her physical cues and practiced grounding techniques to steady herself before responding.

One practice I shared with her:

"Watch a video of yourself in a meeting, with the sound off. What is your face doing when you're not speaking? What does your posture say when you're listening? You may be surprised by what you see."

We reframed listening as an act of leadership, not just courtesy.

"The first reaction sets the tone for everything else," I told her.

"Can you receive even the hard stuff with curiosity instead of contraction?"

As she practiced this, Camille shifted the emotional climate around her. Her team reported feeling more at ease. Trust deepened. And Camille felt less drained because she was no longer in emotional defense mode.

Her gravitas didn't just show up when she spoke. It emerged in how she listened.

In leadership, emotional regulation isn't self-protection—it's how you build trust. When people can predict your emotional tone, they relax and perform.

Listening vs. Waiting to Speak: A Leadership Blind Spot

Camille's story focused on emotional leakage. But there's another form of disconnection that's just as corrosive to trust: pretend listening. That's when a leader appears attentive but is actually planning the next response, rebuttal, or redirect.

I once coached a regional VP who held regular one-on-ones and prided himself on being "a great listener." But feedback from his team painted a different picture.

"He always cuts in before I finish," said one team member.

"It's like he already decided what I meant," according to another.

"Sometimes I just stop talking because I know he's not really taking it in," said yet another.

The disconnect wasn't malicious. It was habitual. We worked to rebuild the muscle of true listening: the kind that suspends judgment, slows down response time, and creates psychological safety.

What gets in the way: listening to fix, defend, or move on.

What builds trust: listening to understand, connect, and build trust.

Great leaders don't listen for the opening to talk. They listen for the moment to elevate others.

That means holding back the "Yes, but" impulse. Your turn will come. Let them land their plane first.

Not every listening challenge shows up in big meetings. For

some leaders, especially those who think fast and feel deeply, the hardest moments are the little ones: pre-meeting chit chat, breakroom banter, small talk in the elevator. It can feel fake, shallow, or just exhausting. But here's the thing: small talk is rarely about the content. It's a warmup. A relational handshake. A way of saying, *I see you*, without diving into your trauma file.

I coach people on this more than you might expect. Surprisingly often, the most brilliant and capable leaders avoid small talk entirely—dismissing it as unnecessary, inefficient, or beneath them. But this "little thing" is a big deal. It builds familiarity. It lowers defenses. It makes rooms feel safer.

If these moments don't come naturally to you, try shifting your focus. You don't need to be entertaining. You just need to be present enough that people feel seen. A simple acknowledgment or curious question can go farther than you think.

Try:

- "What's something you're looking forward to this week?"
- "How's your week unfolding so far?"
- "You always seem calm before these meetings. What's your secret?"

These aren't throwaway lines. They're invitations—gentle signals that say, *I'm paying attention.* That's leadership, too.

So how do you know where your listening falls? One way is to look at the levels of listening and how they land on others.

📌 MODEL: Listening Levels—Passive to Transformational

Here's a quick visual to help you assess how you're showing up in conversations:

LEVEL OF LISTENING	WHAT IT LOOKS LIKE	WHAT IT FEELS LIKE TO OTHERS
1. Passive	Nods, occasional "uh huh," multitasking	Disinterest or dismissal, especially when paired with surface signals like nods or uh huh's that don't match actual engagement. Those sometimes land worse than silence.
2. Reactive	Waiting to speak, frequent interruptions	Defensive or one-upping
3. Active	Paraphrasing, validating, eye contact	Respectful and responsive
4. Empathic	Sensing tone, emotion, reading between lines	Safe and seen
5. Transformational	Full presence, silence, curiosity, deep trust	"You made me feel like I mattered."

Transformational leaders live in Levels 4 and 5.

Yet even when leaders are listening deeply, they have to be mindful of how their listening is read. Linh's story illustrates this.

▶ LINH: The Silence That Spoke Volumes

Linh, a Vice President of Research at a global pharmaceutical company, was known for her sharp scientific acumen and calm, composed leadership. Born and raised in Vietnam, she had moved to the U.S. for her education and had built a thriving global team across three continents.

During a critical product review meeting, an American team member pointed out a significant flaw in the data analysis. Linh nodded, thanked him calmly, and moved on without visible emotion.

Later, her U.S.-based colleagues reported feeling confused and uneasy. "She didn't seem concerned," one said. "It felt like it didn't even register."

Meanwhile, her team members based in Asia had a completely different read: "She was clearly taking it seriously—her pause said everything," one remarked.

In coaching, Linh reflected on how her natural leadership style, rooted in thoughtful reserve and maintaining harmony, was being misinterpreted across cultures.

"In my culture," she explained, "emotional control shows respect and seriousness. But I realize now my American teams need more visible engagement."

We worked on what I call **cultural bridging responses**—simple, authentic ways to visibly acknowledge critical information without abandoning her natural style.

For example, after receiving challenging input, she began saying: "That's important feedback. I'm reflecting on it and we'll address it before the meeting ends."

This small verbal bridge created clarity without forcing her to adopt an inauthentic emotional display. It wasn't about "fixing" her leadership style. It was about making her presence legible across cultures.

Linh's story highlights a bigger truth: cultural expectations shape how presence is read. The same behavior can land very differently, depending on where you are.

FIELD NOTE: Cultural Patterns That Shape Presence

Presence isn't universal. What signals wisdom or maturity in one culture may read as indifference or weakness in another.

CULTURAL DIMENSION	HOW IT AFFECTS PRESENCE	PRACTICAL BRIDGE
High-context versus low-context	In high-context cultures (Japan, China), meaning is conveyed implicitly; in low-context cultures (U.S., Germany), explicit communication is valued.	Name your process: "I'm reflecting on this now."
Emotional expressiveness	Mediterranean and Latin American cultures often value visible passion; Northern European and East Asian cultures often value restraint.	Signal engagement verbally if your natural style is reserved.
Hierarchy orientation	Input is often filtered by perceived status.	Proactively invite input from all levels—especially junior team members who may defer to authority: "I'd specifically like to hear from those closest to the work."

For many leaders, these styles aren't theoretical. They're personal. One leader shared that his father was raised in Iran, where high-context communication was the norm. That shaped his own instincts around nuance, inference, and layered meaning. While it's a gift in many ways, it also created friction when others expected directness or verbal precision. If you've ever been told you're "too vague" or "too intense," it may be a mismatch of cultural expectations—not a reflection of your ability.

Your emotional regulation style isn't right or wrong. But being aware of how it lands across cultural contexts can be the difference between building trust or accidentally creating distance.

► NIKHIL: From Freezing to Steady Presence

Listening isn't just about how you receive others. It also matters when you're the one suddenly expected to respond—clearly, calmly, and in real time.

Nikhil, one of my first coaching clients, was a Senior Director of Data Strategy at a large tech-enabled logistics company. He was smart, meticulous, and deeply respected for his analysis. But when it came to high-stakes, live communication, especially in town halls or leadership meetings, he struggled.

At a quarterly town hall, he was asked an unscripted question about resourcing priorities. He froze. His mind blanked. His thoughts scattered. He passed the mic after offering a few stammered words.

It wasn't catastrophic, but it rattled him.

"You're one of the smartest people here," a peer told him later. "We just need to see it when it counts."

In coaching, we unpacked what happened. Nikhil's nervous system had entered a mild amygdala hijack—the fight-flight-freeze response. Blood flow had shifted away from his logical brain and toward primal defense systems. We worked on spontaneous communication strategies—like keeping two to three go-to talking points ready, using breath to steady his pace, and practicing verbal anchors: short, reliable phrases that could buy time or ease him into clarity.

Phrases like:

- "That's an important point. Let me think that through."
- "Here's how I'm framing it so far."

Over time, the freeze began to ease. But something new emerged.

As Nikhil grew more comfortable speaking in the moment, he noticed a second pattern: When challenged or pushed in a meeting, he didn't freeze. He sharpened. His voice would tighten. His pace would accelerate. He'd overexplain, overcontrol, or clip his tone.

"I don't mean to sound defensive," he said. "But I feel it in my body—this surge of pressure to prove I'm not wrong."

That's where the real work began. Together, we built a tone-awareness practice, one that helped him name what was happening in the moment and regulate before reacting.

We didn't make him less assertive. We helped him lead from steadiness instead of surge.

Now, when faced with challenge, Nikhil pauses. Breathes. Grounds himself. Then he responds with clarity, not control.

His ideas haven't changed. But his energy has. And people feel it.

 ## TOOL: The Four-Second Reset

Nikhil's story shows how pressure can hijack even the sharpest leaders. The good news: you don't have to stay stuck in reaction. A short pause can break the cycle and reset your presence.

When you feel your tone tightening, especially under challenge, try this:

- Breathe (one count): Low and steady. Ground yourself before speaking.
- Anchor (one count): Feel your seat, your feet, your breath. Presence lives in the body.
- Decide (one count): Do I need to respond now, or can I slow the moment?
- Deliver (one count): Speak calmly and directly. No rushing. No flood.

Try reentry phrases like:

- "That's a useful push. Give me a second to think that through."
- "Let me pause before I respond. I want to be sure I'm clear."
- "Here's where I'll start. Then let's build from there."

The Four-Second Reset works as a quick recovery in the moment. But sometimes leaders need a broader set of tools to prepare, anticipate, and respond under sustained pressure.

 TOOL: Under Pressure—A Response Toolkit

Here's a quick-response toolkit I use with clients who tend to freeze, speed up, or emotionally leak under pressure.

1. Bridge phrases (aka verbal airbags):

"That's a complex question—let me take a second to think that through."

"Let me pause before I respond. I want to be thoughtful."

"I want to respond thoughtfully, so here's where I'll begin."

"I'm gathering my thoughts. Give me a moment to frame this."

"Before I jump in, I want to be sure I'm responding clearly."

(Not every moment needs a TED Talk. Sometimes you just need a second to think like a human.)

2. The ready stack: Keep three to five go-to subjects top of mind that apply to almost any question:

- Key business priorities
- Customer needs
- Team development goals

- Culture or team initiatives
- Strategic partnerships
- Opportunities or risks

(Reframing questions into familiar anchors trains your mind to stay centered.)

3. Center then respond: Before responding, try:

- Grounding your feet
- Inhaling deeply
- Relaxing your shoulders

4. Clarify the question (when it's fuzzy):

"Would you mind reframing that?"

"Are you asking about timeline or resourcing?"

"Just to be sure, are you asking for a recommendation or a status update?

"Can I clarify? Is this about immediate impact or long-term outcomes?"

5. Own the pause. Call the pattern:

"You know what? That's not something I've been asked before. Let me think it through."

"You've raised a new angle. I'd like a moment to consider it."

6. Loop back and land:

"Did that land where you were hoping it would?"

"Happy to revisit that if needed."

7. Practice under mild pressure:

Rehearse in front of a colleague. Practice on your commute. Rehearse out loud. Practice being calm as a muscle. Practice brings memory.

Sometimes the pressure doesn't come from the question. It comes from **who's asking it**. A simple ask from a senior leader can trigger a freeze response, even if you know the answer cold.

If this happens, try anchoring to what you already know. Use a bridge phrase like:

- "That's something I've thought about a lot. Give me a second to choose the best example."

- "There are a few angles there. Let me ground us in the take-away."

These aren't stall tactics. They're permission to regulate and respond with presence instead of panic.

Senior leaders often underestimate the emotional weight their presence carries. Even well-intentioned questions can trigger a freeze response if their tone is too sharp or their energy too charged. Warmth isn't weakness. Sometimes the most powerful thing an executive can do is soften the moment—and create space for someone else to rise.

And when stress shows through despite your best efforts, whether it's a clipped tone, a flash of irritation, or a restless pace, what matters is how you recover. The difference between good and great leaders isn't the absence of these moments. It's the way they repair and reset.

► TREY: The Reset That Rebuilt Trust

Trey, a Chief Marketing Officer at a fast-growing consumer brand, prided himself on his even temperament. He was known for his calm demeanor and steady leadership style, even when things got messy.

But during a particularly intense product launch, after multiple delays, back-to-back meetings, and a late-night scramble, Trey lost his cool. Mid-meeting, when his creative director suggested yet another round of changes, Trey snapped. The frustration came out sharp and fast—in front of the entire team.

The moment passed quickly. Trey kept going as if nothing had happened. But something had shifted. Over the next few days, he noticed a subtle change in the team. They were more hesitant in meetings. A little less forthcoming with challenges. A little more careful with their words.

In our coaching session, we unpacked what had happened.

"I thought since I didn't make a big deal of it, they'd forget it," he said.

I reflected back: "That moment wasn't minor to them. It was revealing—because it was rare."

Trey wasn't a reactive leader. That's why it stood out. **Executive emotions hold disproportionate weight.** One flash of frustration from someone in his position lands differently. It signals more than stress. It changes the temperature of the room.

Trey didn't need to overcorrect. But he did need to repair the relational field.

We used a simple protocol I call the **Three-Part Recovery**—a reset tool I teach for exactly this kind of moment.

1. **Acknowledge:** Name the emotional moment without overexplaining.

2. **Reset:** Reconnect briefly and sincerely.

3. **Rebuild:** Show consistent, regulated presence moving forward.

Trey started with a short, direct acknowledgment at his next team meeting:

"I want to address something. Last week, I responded sharply during our creative review. That wasn't about your work. It was about *my* stress level. It wasn't my best moment, and it is certainly not how I would like to lead."

He didn't dwell on it. He didn't over apologize. He simply named it, owned it, and moved forward.

The effect was immediate. By saying what everyone had felt but no one had named, Trey didn't lose credibility. He amplified it.

This was gravitas in action and a Second Circle moment. Calm, attuned, and relational—the kind of grounded presence we explored in the last chapter. Performance fades. Bravado cracks. What lasts is composure under fire.

The Ripple Effect of Recovery

When a leader circles back after a misstep, whether it's a sharp tone, a reactive decision, or a moment of emotional leakage, the recovery often lands louder than the mistake.

It signals self-awareness. It builds trust. It invites others back into the relationship.

But here's the nuance: most people don't expect perfection from their leaders. What they're scanning for is presence—especially when things go sideways.

The moments you reenter with clarity, accountability, or curiosity don't just repair. They lead.

Here's what different recovery moves communicate, whether you say them out loud or not:

RESPONSE TO EMOTIONAL LEAKAGE	WHAT IT COMMUNICATES
"Let me rephrase that. What I meant to say was…"	I'm present and responsible for my words.
"I realize that might have landed wrong."	I'm aware of my tone and impact.
A pause followed by a calmer reentry	I'm regulating myself in real time.
Circling back after a meeting to clarify or repair	I value the relationship more than being right.

Every one of these micro resets helps reshape your leadership brand—not as someone who avoids pressure but as someone who knows how to navigate it.

TOOL: Daily Warm-Up

Resilient leaders don't just react to pressure; they prime themselves for it. One practice I recommend to clients is **the commute warm-up.** On your way to work (or just before a big meeting), practice answering two or three questions out loud that you could realistically be asked on the spot:

- What's one strategic priority we're tackling this quarter?
- How are we managing resources right now?
- Where are we seeing traction—and what's next?

It's like running scales before performing. You remind your brain that you're ready.

FIELD NOTE: Who Gets Grace Under Pressure?

Real-time reaction and response is not judged equally. Professionals from historically marginalized groups, especially women and BIPOC leaders, often face higher expectations for composure, polish, and emotional regulation. Pauses may be read as indecision. Firmness may be read as aggression.

Cultural norms matter, too. In some cultures, a thoughtful pause is seen as wise. In others, it's mistaken for a lack of preparation.

And for Gen Z and younger Millennials—raised in digital, asynchronous environments—live dialogue can feel unfamiliar and create unexpected stress. Written fluency doesn't always translate to verbal agility. That doesn't mean they lack depth. It means the channel is unfamiliar.

SPIRITUAL CUE: Fear as an Opening

Across traditions, fear is not a flaw but a signal. Ram Dass described it as a moment of separation, where the ego grasps for control. The remedy? Presence.

The Bhagavad Gita teaches right speech: timely, calm, truthful, necessary. In the Gospels, Jesus often paused before responding—offering presence before solution.

Great leaders learn to recognize fear, not as a weakness but as an invitation to lead from their center.

Ask: *Can I meet this moment with composure, not protection? Am I speaking from reaction or from grounded focus?*

READER-TO-LEADER

Reflect:

- What do others notice first about me when I'm under pressure?

- How often do I confuse reacting quickly with leading well?

- Where could a pause shift my impact this week?

Act:

- Choose one bridge phrase this week, e.g., "Let's slow down and think this through," or "I'd like to hear more before we decide."

- Before your next high-stakes meeting, pause to anchor with one breath or grounding gesture before you answer.

- Ask a trusted colleague to role-play unexpected questions, and pay attention to your first reactions.

REMEMBER THIS: *In leadership, pause is power.*

SPEAK TO LEAD

The Visibility Accelerator

There's no faster way to raise your leadership stock price than by giving a great presentation—and then following it up with another and another.

One strong moment at the front of the room can shift how people see you and what conversations you get invited into afterward. It can spark reputational ripple effects, shift your perceived readiness, and accelerate your visibility across the organization. It's not just about the content. It's about the energy you transmit—and the clarity others feel when you speak.

Yet, too many great leaders avoid the spotlight. They freeze. They overscript. They chase perfection instead of connection. They wait to feel ready. Or they speak, but they don't land.

This chapter is about changing that. The room is already watching. The question is: What are you going to do with the mic?

The Fear Layer

For many high achievers, public speaking doesn't feel like a growth moment. It feels like exposure. And if you're carrying early memories of being judged, overlooked, or misread, the front of the room feels like a risk you'd rather not take.

For those from underrepresented groups, the front of the room can carry even more weight—not just visibility, but extra scrutiny. That fear isn't weakness. It's experience.

But what if that fear is the doorway?

As we saw with Nikhil and Angela in earlier chapters, the shift doesn't come from erasing fear. It comes from learning to regulate your system, claim your insight, and show up with clarity anyway.

Speaking is presence work. And presence work is leadership work.

Why Speaking Changes the Game

Whether your audience is five or five thousand, the fundamentals don't change. Strip it down, and speaking comes down to three things: Did they understand you? Did they feel you? Did they want more from you?

When you speak—in a meeting, at a town hall, on stage— you're not just conveying content. You're shaping:

- How people perceive your readiness
- What tone others follow
- Whether your ideas travel across rooms
- Whether others sponsor, elevate, or echo you

One client put it this way: "The moment I nailed that presentation, people started treating me like a VP—long before the title followed."

Here's the loop:

Speak → Be Seen → Be Invited → Speak Again

Most promotions are discussed in rooms you don't control. But the impression others carry of you? That starts in the front of the room.

And let me say this clearly: while there are plenty of excellent books, classes, and resources available to improve your public speaking, this chapter is not a replacement for those. I encourage every client to seek out every possible avenue to strengthen this skill. But I also believe it's such a pivotal area of growth that I dedicate time to it in every coaching engagement—*whether or not* public speaking was part of the original remit. If I'm working with a leader, at some point, we're going to work on how they show up and speak when it matters most.

Because when you do it well, you're not just giving a presentation—you're building a fan base. You're scaling your leadership brand.

MODEL: The Visibility Loop

I often describe this progression as the **Visibility Loop**—the speaking flywheel that builds momentum over time.

Speak: Show insight, presence, and energy that matches your intent.

Be Seen: Decision-makers, peers, and skip-level leaders take notice.

Be Invited: You're asked to present again, speak for your function, or brief up.

Speak Again: Your reputation compounds, credibility rises.

This is how visibility builds. Speak well, be seen, and momentum takes care of the rest.

A Small Talk Can Spark a Shift

Danielle was a highly capable operations manager known for her sharp execution, but she avoided public speaking at all costs. "I'd rather fight fires behind the scenes than take the mic," she once joked in session.

But when she was asked to give a short update at a divisional review, we worked together on one key shift: a breath reset before stepping up. We also worked on using one clear **"money phrase"—that memorable line she could land with complete confidence.**

The result? The update was short—just five minutes—but senior leaders took notice. One invited her to co-lead a cross-functional pilot. That moment became the first domino in a long chain of increased visibility.

She didn't master public speaking overnight. But she stopped waiting to be ready—and that changed everything.

Some speaking moments are quick sparks that open doors. Others demand more—the shaping, rehearsal, and rigor needed to leave a lasting mark.

FIELD NOTE: The Work Behind the Wow

One of my clients, Gary—already an experienced speaker—was tapped to give a TEDx talk. Just 12 minutes long.

We worked together five times over three months. And he worked hard in between. Each session, we refined his message, polished the flow, strengthened the emotional resonance, and calibrated his gestures and vocal delivery. Why? Because that talk would live online forever. And he wanted it to reflect not just his insight, but his presence.

Here's what I tell every client: Great talks aren't just written. They're built. Polished. Practiced.

Public speaking experts estimate that a strong 30-minute

talk may take 15 to 30 hours of preparation. A keynote? Easily 40 to 100 hours across research, design, storytelling, and rehearsal.

This isn't meant to scare you. It's meant to normalize the effort that excellence requires.

You don't need this level of rigor for every update. But when the stakes are high, your preparation should match.

What Undermines Great Speaking

Even when the message is strong, a few common habits can weaken delivery. These are all fixable—but only if you know to look for them:

- Over-prepping the script, under-prepping the presence
- Speeding through content instead of landing key moments
- Letting fear drive filler words, shallow breath, or robotic tone
- Mistaking detail for credibility, instead of clarity for impact

And the most common trap? Spending hours tweaking slides—fonts, bullets, transitions—while skipping the real work. Instead of staring at the deck, invest your prep time in:

- Rehearsing vocal inflection
- Tightening your core message
- Finding the emotional hook
- Practicing how you show up, not just what you show

The deck is not the delivery. **You** are the delivery.
(You'll find a full toolkit for vocal presence in Appendix I.)

The Three Purposes of a Strong Talk

When I coach clients for big presentations, I ask them to focus on three goals:

1. **Inform**

   Share the solid data. Make the business case. Give the audience something valuable to think about.

2. **Entertain**

   This doesn't mean jokes or gimmicks, especially if that's not your strength. It means being human. Dynamic. Alive. Use vocal range, facial expression, movement, and presence. How your audience *experiences you* is what keeps them with you.

3. **Inspire**

   Give people something to *do* or *believe in*. Create uplift. Offer a clear next step or vision. Inspire the room to act, not just nod.

When your talk does all three, it becomes **memorable**. Repeatable. Impactful.

And here's the part I make clear to every client: **You don't have to be perfect.** Audiences are remarkably forgiving of visible nerves, stumbling over words, or forgetting a point and circling back to it. **But there are two things they will not forgive you for:**

> DO NOT bore them.
> DO NOT waste their time.

No one has ever walked out of a presentation and said, "I wish that had been longer."

What's boring? It's rarely the content—if it matters to the business, it matters. But *you* will be boring if your energy is flat, your tone is monotone, your delivery robotic. If your presence doesn't match your message, people disconnect.

And wasting their time? That's about knowing your audience. Give them what *they* need. Tailor your message. When you land with energy and clarity, the room doesn't just listen. They want you back. That's how a fan base begins.

Second Circle Energy—Where Resonance Lives

You discovered voice coach and performance master Patsy Rodenburg's work earlier in this book, when we explored the Three Circles of Energy as a lens for confidence and embodied leadership. But nowhere is this model more vivid—or more essential—than when you're standing at the front of the room.

- First Circle collapses inward: hesitant, often overly rehearsed, trying to disappear. The audience feels the retreat.

- Third Circle blasts outward: performative, pushy, impressive at first but overwhelming over time.

- Second Circle is the sweet spot. You're focused and attuned, speaking with the room, not at it. Your energy lands—and it comes back to you.

When a speaker is in Second Circle, it feels intimate, even in a ballroom. People lean in. They trust you. And they remember how you made them feel.

Great speakers don't overpower. They don't disappear. They transmit.

Why this matters for leadership: While Rodenburg framed Second Circle as a performance tool, I have found it to be the defining state of modern leadership presence. Leaders who learn to anchor here don't just deliver content—they **create resonance**, the steady relational energy that builds trust and amplifies influence.

 COACHING CUE: Notice when you tip out of Second Circle and shrink back into First or push into Third. The reset isn't about performance. It's about recalibration.

What To Do About Nervousness

Nervousness isn't a flaw. It's an energy surge. Your job isn't to suppress it. It's to **rechannel** it.

Here's what I tell clients:

- Don't try to be calm. Try to be clear.
- Don't try to be fearless. Try to be present.
- Don't try to hide your nerves. Try to regulate your breath.

Your body is doing something real. Work with it. Speak from your feet. Breathe. Make eye contact.

Then keep going.

FIELD NOTE: When Nerves Take Over the Room

I still get nervous before a high-stakes talk. Not because I'm unprepared, but because I care. That energy shows up in my body as elevated heart rate, tighter breath, and sometimes, yes, shaky hands.

I've even knocked over a glass of water at the podium. It wasn't from panic, but from that subtle mismatch between brain and body when I wasn't fully oxygenated. It happens when your system is in go mode, but your breath hasn't caught up.

That's what nerves do. They scramble the connection between intention and execution.

But here's the truth: nerves are fuel. They mean your system is online. When you know how to work with them—breathe, ground, and stay relational—that energy becomes presence.

I don't aim for calm anymore. I aim for clear. For connected. For ready.

TOOLS THAT WORK: Real-Time Speaking Presence

Whether you're stepping into a boardroom, logging into a high-stakes call, or giving a keynote, your presence is the delivery. These tools help you lead the moment, not just survive it.[4]

- Breathe on purpose beforehand: Use the Four-Point Frequency Reset—inhale, hold, exhale, stillness. It brings your system online and recenters your energy.

- Name your cue word: Choose one word that anchors you (e.g., steady, generous, clear). Repeat it silently as you breathe.

- Take a moment before you begin: Pause, make eye contact, and smile. Let the room settle. Your first look says, "This is going to mean something."

- Speak from your feet: Stand or sit tall. Let your weight drop into your base. Stability transmits.

- Make contact: Look at one person. Then another. Connection is built one face at a time.

- Slow your start: Don't rush to fill the silence. Let the pause add weight to your presence.

- Center your message: What do they need to hear and what do you want them to feel? Speak from there.

- Nail your open and close: The first minute and final 20 seconds are your most powerful moments. Your audience is deciding whether to trust you, listen to you, and remember you. Consider memorizing your opening lines so you can deliver them with full presence. A strong opening helps you regulate your own nerves while assuring your audience you have things well in hand. End with clarity: Close with a

---

4 **Want to go deeper?** See Appendix I on "Vocal Presence and Executive Voice" for techniques to expand your range, deliver your "money phrase," and increase your impact.

message, a call to action, or a clear invitation. Pause. Smile. Thank them for listening, and leave them wanting more.

- Start small and start often: If the stage feels too big right now, practice in lower-stakes spaces, for instance, team check-ins, one-on-ones, brief meeting openers, moderating a panel or introducing a colleague. Repetition rewires the fear and builds the muscle.

- Stay in Second Circle: Don't shrink back. Don't put on a show. Stay present and connected.

And remember—"front of room" isn't always a stage. Today it might be Zoom square, a hybrid pane, or a webinar with faces you can't even see. The same rules apply: breathe, ground, and connect one person at a time. Look into the lens the way you'd hold someone's eyes across a table. Even through a screen, presence travels.

FIELD NOTE: Beyond the Org Chart

Elena was a senior HR manager at a manufacturing company. She was respected internally but overlooked for bigger roles. A colleague encouraged her to join a panel at a regional HR association conference.

She hesitated. Speaking had always made her anxious. But over the past year, she'd been quietly attending Toastmasters, working on her confidence in front of a room. The panel became her chance to put that practice to work.

The event became a turning point. Her insights were quoted in industry blogs. Two board members in her own company mentioned hearing about her session. And a year later, she was approached by a global competitor to lead talent strategy—an offer that doubled her scope.

Inside her company, Elena had blended into the background. On stage, she was suddenly visible. The opportunity didn't come from working harder in the office. It came from speaking where the right people could hear her.

Try this: Say yes to one panel, one workshop, one association roundtable. Use it as practice, not performance. Your next opportunity may not come from the room you're in today—it may come from the stage you're willing to step onto.

READER-TO-LEADER: Lead From the Front

Reflect:

- When have I spoken in a way that made others see me differently?
- What gets in the way of saying yes to the front of the room?
- What would change if I stopped avoiding the mic?

Act:

- Record a two-minute take on a topic you know well. Watch it back with curiosity.
- Choose one technique from this chapter to try this week (money phrase, breath reset, etc.)
- Say yes to one speaking opportunity that stretches you, and prepare with intention.

SPIRITUAL CUE: Voice as Transmission

In many spiritual traditions, the spoken word is transmission, not just sound.

The Gospel of John begins: "In the beginning was the Word." In Hindu philosophy, the syllable *aum* is not just a sound, it's the vibration of universal presence. Across cultures, language has always been a carrier of energetic intent.

When you speak from Second Circle—grounded, clear,

attuned—you don't just share information. You create resonance.

Your voice doesn't need to be perfect. It needs to be true.

Let your speaking presence be a form of leadership transmission, not to dominate, but to serve.

> **REMEMBER THIS:** *If presence is your leadership currency, then speaking is your investment vehicle.*
>
> *Get visible. Get heard. Then get invited back.*

COACHING AS CULTURE

Growing People, Not Just Results

Culture is shaped by what leaders tolerate—and what they model. That's why so many companies update systems and strategies as they grow, but many forget to update how they lead. That gap can sabotage everything else.

This is the difference: some organizations operate from a culture of control, where leaders prize loyalty, respect, and predictability. Others build a culture of coaching, where leaders grow people as intentionally as they grow results.

The first model protects power. The second multiplies it.

This chapter is about that shift—why it matters, what it looks like, and how to lead it.

► ARJUN: When Leadership Stays in the Family

Arjun was the third-generation leader of a privately held, family-run manufacturing company. Over the past fifteen years, the business had scaled across multiple states, adding professional layers to what was once a lean family operation. On paper, it looked like a success story. But inside, frustration was simmering.

Arjun and his two siblings still made all the big decisions. Their leadership style was authoritative—decisive, loyal, and deeply personal. They prided themselves on taking care of employees and maintaining the legacy their grandfather started. But they didn't trust outsiders easily, and they especially didn't value dissent.

When a rising executive—one of the company's first external hires—brought me in for coaching, the goal was to help him "navigate the family." As I started my discovery process, I heard the same feedback across the board:

- "No one gives real feedback around here."
- "You just have to figure out what they want."
- "They say they want input. But when you give it, it's seen as disrespect."

The most dangerous part? Arjun and his siblings had no idea. They believed they were approachable. They believed they were mentoring. In reality, they were stifling growth.

This is what happens where coaching is treated as a fix-it tool for underperformers, a checkbox during review season, or a vague HR concept floated at off-sites.

But in the most forward-thinking organizations, coaching is something else entirely:

- It's a daily posture of leadership.
- It's a language spoken at every level.
- It's a mindset that shifts from judging to developing.
- Most important, coaching creates feedback flow, not just feedback loops.

No amount of operational scaling would fix what was stuck

at the core until that shift occurred. Without a cultural reset, growth stalls. Coaching isn't just a tool—it's the reset that keeps pace with disruption.

In a coaching culture:

- Feedback moves up, down, and across.
- Leaders are expected to grow others, not just manage performance.
- Mistakes are mined for learning, not blame.
- Power is shared, not hoarded.

That's the shift Arjun's company needed but couldn't yet see.

MODEL: Five Coaching Shifts for Executives

Many executives are promoted for their ability to fix problems, make tough calls, and drive results. But the higher you go, the less useful those habits become. Leadership shifts from doing to developing. From producing outcomes to growing capacity.

A senior exec once told me, half-joking, "I've basically become the company help desk. Everyone brings me problems and waits for me to fix them."

It was a laugh—but also the problem. She was still operating like the smartest person in the room instead of the coach of the room. Her default was fixing, not developing.

Here are five coaching shifts every executive must make:

1. **From performance judgment to growth orientation**
   Lead with curiosity, not correction. Ask: "What can we learn from this?"

2. **From telling to asking**
   Great coaches ask questions that create thinking. Try: "What options have you considered?" or "What would success look like here?"

3. **From heroism to multiplier mindset**
   Don't be the fixer; build fixers. Your influence scales when your people do.

4. **From protecting power to sharing power**
   Invite others into decision-making. Ownership grows where trust is given.

5. **From episodic feedback to ongoing dialogue**
   Feedback isn't a one-time event. It's a conversation that moves in every direction.

REDEFINING COACHING: From Punishment to Potential

In many legacy companies, "coaching" has a bad brand. It's often linked to performance improvement plans or whispered behind closed doors as a warning: "You're about to be managed out."

This outdated framing treats coaching as a remedial tool for people who aren't cutting it.

But in modern leadership, coaching isn't about what's broken. It's about what's becoming. When coaching becomes cultural, it signals investment, not intervention. It's a way of saying: "We believe in your growth and we see your future."

And make no mistake: coaching cultures aren't soft. They raise the bar. A McKinsey study found that organizations with strong feedback and coaching cultures outperform peers in innovation, retention, and financial performance.

Why? Because coaching cultures:

- Shift accountability from top-down pressure to shared responsibility.
- Build internal bench strength and reduce dependency.
- Give senior executives honest insight, something rare at the top.

If you want leaders who can think, stretch, and scale, don't manage them. Coach them.

What Coaching Sounds Like

Inspired in part by the work of Michael Bungay Stanier's *The Coaching Habit*, this section offers practical coaching behaviors that require no certification, just intention.

What coaching often sounds like:

- "What are you learning from this experience?"
- "What would success look like here?"
- "If I weren't here, how would you handle it?"
- "Who else should be part of this conversation?"
- "Tell me more about how you landed on that decision."

These questions:

- Shift accountability back to the team.
- Build critical thinking and decision-making.
- Signal belief in the other person's capacity.

Pro tip: Culture shifts one question at a time: Don't wait for permission—start by asking better questions.

► ALEX: The Move from Fixer to Coach

Alex was a Vice President of Merchandising for a major national retailer. A sharp, instinctive merchant, he made fast decisions and got results. His team knew he'd step in when things got stuck, and he often did, whether they asked or not.

But as his role expanded, so did the strain. "I'm spending too much time solving other people's problems," he admitted. "I want to build leaders, not babysit issues."

We began working on the shift from fixer to coach. He started holding space in one-on-ones, asking instead of telling, creating room for others to step up.

One of his direct reports, Tina, did step up. At first, she hesitated because she was accustomed to Alex's hands-on style. But with time, she began showing up differently: clear framing, better analysis, real ownership. Within six months, she was leading a key vendor transformation project and mentoring two junior managers.

Then there was Ryan. On paper, he was capable. But in practice, he was coaching Teflon; everything slid off.

Alex tried again and again. He asked open-ended questions. Ryan agreed—then came back with the same problem. Alex invited reflection. Ryan nodded—then redirected the question back to Alex. Alex offered choice points: "Which option would you take?" Ryan deflected: "What do you think?"

On the surface, Ryan looked cooperative. In reality, he was doing just enough to avoid accountability. Every conversation felt like a reset to zero.

That's when Alex realized: coaching only works if both parties are invested. Ryan wanted convenience, not growth. At that point, leadership became about clarity, not rescue. Alex set expectations, reinforced follow-through, and when Ryan still didn't engage, he helped him exit the team.

Tina stayed. And grew. So did the team. And so did Alex.

Because coaching isn't just about helping individuals evolve. It's a strategic leadership filter. Leaders who coach spot who's ready to rise, see who's stuck in resistance, and build teams that understand what leadership looks like.

Coaching isn't a replacement for management. Expectations, follow-up, and clarity are the foundation. Coaching adds the inner work: reflection, self-awareness, and choice. When that doesn't land—**it's okay to lead, not coach.**

► TOMAS: When a Team Learns to Speak Up

Tomas was the CEO of a regional healthcare system—sharp, metrics-driven, and respected for his operational steadiness. He led a senior team of clinical and administrative leaders who were capable, loyal, and a little too quiet.

When Tomas brought me in as a coach, he believed the team was aligned. "They do what I ask," he said. "But I wish they'd be more proactive—challenge ideas, think ahead of the curve."

During discovery interviews, the truth emerged. One team member described Tomas as "clear but hard to read." Another admitted, "I give him the answer I know he wants. Then I fix the real issue later."

Tomas wasn't a bad leader. He just wasn't getting feedback because his team didn't know if it was safe.

Over the next six months, we worked on embedding coaching practices into his executive rhythm, not just in one-on-ones, but in group dynamics. Tomas began asking different questions:

- "What are we not naming yet?"
- "What concerns are still in the room?"
- "If this plan fails, what will we wish someone had said?"

He opened strategic planning sessions with reflection. He ended exec meetings with unfiltered debriefs. He rotated facilitation roles so that every leader owned the room at least once a quarter.

It didn't happen overnight. But by the end of the year, the climate had shifted. Debates got sharper, peer coaching emerged, and one leader said, "I no longer edit myself in his presence."

That's when I knew: Tomas didn't just change how he led. He changed what and how the team spoke. Coaching became the new dialect.

Still, not every moment calls for coaching. Sometimes, leaders need to shift gears and instead offer clarity, direction, or decision-making.

FIELD NOTE: Coaching Isn't Always the Answer

Coaching is powerful. But it's not universal. It's not always the right move in real time.

Coaching may backfire:

- When a direct report is overwhelmed and needs clarity, not open-ended questions
- When someone is in active resistance or deflection mode
- When the issue at hand is compliance, safety, or legal risk
- When the leader is exhausted or dysregulated and can't offer a stable, safe space for dialogue

In those moments, the coaching mindset still matters, but the move may need to shift:

- From inquiry to clarity
- From space-holding to structure
- From development to decision

And sometimes the right adjustment is in how you frame the question itself:

- "Would it help to explore that together?"
- "This might be outside my lane, but here's what I'm wondering..."

Coaching isn't about asking clever questions for the sake of it. It's about asking the right question, in the right spirit, at the right moment.

Embedding Coaching Culture

Coaching culture doesn't happen through slogans or posters. It's built through consistent actions, modeled in your daily leadership and reinforced by the systems around you.

Ask yourself: Am I contributing to this kind of culture or unintentionally sustaining the one I say I want to change?

Leadership actions. These are the daily habits and signals your team watches for.

- Do I praise progress out loud—or only perfection?
- Do I give feedback regularly—or save it for formal reviews?
- Do I make space for reflection in meetings and one-on-ones—or rush for answers?
- Do I ask open-ended questions before offering advice?
- Am I encouraging peer feedback and accountability, or doing all the lifting myself?

System anchors. Culture doesn't shift by good intentions alone. It takes reinforcement.

- Do our performance systems reward development—or just outcomes?
- Do leaders at every level get measured on how well they grow others?
- Do our processes encourage feedback across, not just down?
- Do performance reviews build learning—or only tally results?

Culture doesn't change through intention alone. It shifts through repetition. Once you've seeded the coaching mindset at the systems level, the next step is personal: how you show up in everyday moments.

TOOL: Everyday Coaching Habits That Shift Culture

You don't need a title change or a program to lead with a coaching posture. These three everyday habits—when modeled consistently—create cultural shift, one conversation at a time.

1. **Model the reflective pause**. Don't rush to fill silence. Pause. Let the question hang. It shows you're thinking and it teaches others to think, too. In a fast-moving culture, a thoughtful pause is a leadership signal.

2. **Ask one more question**. When someone finishes talking, don't pivot to your point. Ask: "What else do you see?" or "Is there a part you haven't named yet?" The second question is often where the real insight lives. Asking one more doesn't slow the conversation. It deepens it.

3. **Practice the coach-back.** When someone brings you a challenge, don't solve it immediately. Ask them to return with three options—even rough ones. "Bring me what you'd do if I weren't here." Over time, this habit builds ownership, autonomy, and strategic thinking—the cultural currency of a coach-led team.

In a disrupted world, culture is the ultimate reset. Systems may shift, strategy may pivot, but leaders who coach create the resilience.

READER-TO-LEADER: Start Building the Culture

You don't need a certification to lead like a coach. Start here.

Reflect:

- Where am I still defaulting to telling, when I could be asking?
- What would shift if I slowed my feedback to include more curiosity?
- How am I modeling the mindset I want my team to embody?
- Which coaching habits (pause, ask one more question, coachback) will I model this week?

Act:

- Shift one conversation from advice-giving to curiosity.
- Lead one meeting this week with a coaching posture.
- Prepare two open-ended questions in advance.

Afterward, reflect: What shifted? What did I learn about my team's thinking?

FIELD NOTE: What Coaching Is Not

Before we leave this topic, let's clear up a few myths:

- Coaching is not therapy. It's future-focused and action-oriented.

- Coaching is not micromanagement. It builds independence, not dependence.

- Coaching is not a remedial tool. It's how high-potential talent grows.

SPIRITUAL CUE: The Wisdom of Connection

Through Jane Roberts, the teacher known as Seth taught that "you create your own reality." That's exactly what coaching cultures do: they shape conditions where growth becomes possible, not forced.

Zen teacher Thich Nhat Hanh called it "deep listening"—a form of presence that helps others discover their own answer, not by being told what to do, but by being heard well enough to remember who they are.

Quaker educator Parker Palmer reminds us that leadership is not about technique. It's about integrity. "It comes from the inwardness out of which we live," he wrote.

Coaching leadership doesn't begin with a method. It begins with presence.

These teachings converge on one point: real transformation doesn't come from control.

It comes from the quiet strength to hold space—without fixing, without performing, without proving.

Leadership that grows others begins with this question: Can I create the kind of space where someone else can hear their own wisdom?

REMEMBER THIS: *You don't have to shift the whole system today. You just have to grow it—one brave, curious conversation at a time.*

THE MIND FLIP

From Problems to Polarities

Think of the hardest decision you've faced as a leader. Was it really a problem to solve—or a tension you had to hold?

Most leaders are trained to fix problems: See the issue, resolve it, move on. That formula works beautifully for many challenges. But at higher levels, some of the most critical decisions stop acting like problems. They come back. They clash. They refuse to be "fixed."

Welcome to the Tension

Imagine this scene: your team is divided. Half argues passionately for greater innovation and risk-taking. The other half demands stability and operational excellence. As the leader, you're stuck in the middle, feeling the pressure to pick a side.

Sound familiar? What if trying to solve this situation is your first mistake?

But some forces in leadership are not puzzles with a correct answer. They're opposing truths that need to be held at the same time. Innovation versus efficiency. Centralization versus autonomy. Short-term gains versus long-term value.

These aren't problems. They're polarities—two essential forces that must be navigated together. This ability to hold tension rather than collapse into one side is part of the Hidden Job Description we explored in Chapter 4. As leaders rise, they're evaluated less on fixing problems and more on their capacity to hold polarities in creative tension.

► SARAH: The Innovation Trap

Sarah, a CEO I've worked with for years, was exasperated when I first introduced this idea.

"So you're telling me I need to find the balance? That's not exactly revolutionary advice."

"Not balance," I told her. "Dynamic navigation. And the revolution isn't in what you do—it's in how you think."

She gave me the "That's it?" face. Every coach knows that face. But that's the pivot—the shift from solving to sensing.

This is what I call the **Mind Flip**—the moment when an executive stops treating tension like a problem to solve and starts recognizing it as a polarity to lead through.

Polarity example: Innovation vs. efficiency

To navigate tensions more consciously, it helps to map them visually. Here's one of the most common polarities:

INNOVATION	EFFICIENCY
Fuels growth, energy, creativity	Fuels clarity, margin, consistency
Drives risk-taking and disruption	Drives discipline and operational excellence
Downsides: Chaos, rework, lack of focus	Downsides: Stagnation, bureaucracy, resistance to change

Leadership cue: Don't choose one. Navigate both by flexing your emphasis based on context, timing, and strategic goals.

Polarity example: Autonomy vs. alignment

Another polarity that surfaces constantly—especially at higher levels—is autonomy versus alignment.

AUTONOMY	ALIGNMENT
Fuels innovation, ownership, speed	Fuels cohesion, clarity, scale
Empowers local decision-making	Ensures unified brand and enterprise consistency
Downsides: Silos, misalignment	Downsides: Bureaucracy, slow decision-making

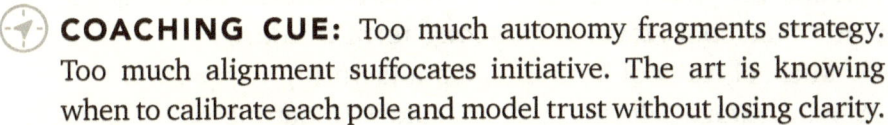 **COACHING CUE:** Too much autonomy fragments strategy. Too much alignment suffocates initiative. The art is knowing when to calibrate each pole and model trust without losing clarity.

FIELD NOTE: Matrixed Cultures Magnify Polarity

In a matrixed organization, leaders often report to multiple stakeholders—for example, as a business unit leader and a functional head. This design is meant to drive cross-functional leverage and strategic alignment. But it also creates friction:

- Business unit leaders prioritize speed and local autonomy.
- Functional leaders emphasize standardization and enterprise consistency.

If you're an executive inside a matrix, you live this polarity daily. Success isn't about picking a side. It's about learning to:

- Translate. Connecting enterprise priorities to local realities.

- Negotiate. Surfacing tensions early, framing tradeoffs explicitly.
- Navigate. Flex based on context, timing, and stakes.

Matrix leadership demands high-polarity literacy. Collapse fully into autonomy, and the enterprise fragments. Collapse fully into alignment, and innovation dies.

Great leaders don't "solve" these tensions. They become fluent polarity navigators—especially in complex, matrixed systems.

COACHING CUE: If you keep trying to fix something that won't go away—it's probably not a problem. It's a polarity.

The Tension Between Results and Resilience

Perhaps no polarity challenges modern leaders more consistently than **short-term versus long-term thinking.**

Michael, CEO of a midsize manufacturing company with a 75-year history, felt this tension acutely. Under increasing pressure from activist investors, he had spent three years relentlessly focusing on efficiency: cutting costs, reducing headcount, consolidating facilities, and boosting margins.

On paper, it worked: stock up, profits up.

But when we began coaching, Michael confessed something troubling: "I'm hitting all my targets, but I'm hollowing out the company. We've cut training. Innovation has stalled. Our best people are leaving. I'm not building—I'm harvesting."

He had overweighted short-term results, serving current investors while undermining the long-term vitality of the business.

Polarity Example: Short-term results vs. long-term sustainability

OVEREMPHASIS ON SHORT TERM	HEALTHY RHYTHM	OVEREMPHASIS ON LONG TERM
Fuels quick wins, meets investor expectations	Strategic pacing with visible milestones	Avoids urgency; may delay key decisions
Delivers measurable outcomes fast	Builds sustainable capacity	Prioritizes vision over execution
Burnout, innovation decline, and reactive culture	Balances performance and resilience	Progress may stall without visible wins

He didn't "fix" the short-term focus. He started naming it. He opened team meetings by acknowledging the sprint for profits—and clarifying what would follow it. He led differently because he was thinking differently.

The Integration Path

Most polarity coaching doesn't end with balance. It ends with integration.

The goal isn't to sit in the middle. It's to build fluency between the poles. Great leaders flex intentionally, explain why, and stay grounded in the larger purpose.

Michael didn't abandon performance. But he began actively managing the polarity by:

- Adding metrics for employee development, innovation pipeline, and cultural health.
- Shifting the conversation from quarterly scorecards to "horizon reporting" across short-, mid-, and long-term outcomes.
- Training his team in polarity thinking to avoid sliding too far into either extreme.

The turning point came when he told the entire company: "We're building something here, not just for this quarter or this year, but for the next generation. That means we need both performance now and capacity for the future."

Integration isn't neutrality. It's maturity.

COACHING CUE: Holding tension like this requires presence—not pressure. It's a Second Circle skill: grounded, relational, steady. The most dangerous polarities are the ones you can't see—until you've drifted too far in one direction. And once you've learned to navigate them yourself, the next challenge is helping your team do it together. That's culture-shaping.

► **KARINA: From Polarity War to Polarity Wisdom**

Karina led digital transformation at a large insurance firm. Her team, known for its rigor and depth, insisted on building a fully integrated, secure, and scalable platform before any rollout.

"We can't afford a weak launch," one of the architects said. "If we cut corners now, we'll just pay for it later."

Meanwhile, the marketing team was pushing hard for early releases and rapid iteration. "We don't need perfect—we need progress," their VP countered.

The debates were heated. Meetings stalled. People began to take sides. And the project was stuck because of competing commitments.

In coaching, Karina saw it clearly: this wasn't a problem with a right answer. It was a polarity: comprehensive quality versus speed to market. Her leadership move wasn't to decide which side should win. It was to help the team hold the tension well.

Karina guided the team through a simple process:

- Name the tension.
- Acknowledge the value in both perspectives.
- Surface the risks of favoring either side.
- Build rituals to keep polarity awareness alive.

Weekly "polarity checks" became their new leadership rhythm. The approach that emerged integrated both priorities into a single path forward.

- Core security and data infrastructure would be built comprehensively.
- Customer-facing features would be released in rapid, iterative cycles.
- Weekly "polarity checks" would assess if they were tilting too far in either direction.

The impact went beyond this single project. Team members who had previously seen each other as obstacles now recognized they were simply holding complementary values. The "us versus them" dynamic shifted to a "both/and" mindset.

Teams don't need to agree on everything. They need a shared language for productively holding tension. When you teach polarity thinking, you don't just resolve conflict—you upgrade your team's ability to handle complexity.

FIELD NOTE: Recognizing a Polarity in Real Time

External tension is often just a mirror of internal conflict. The real work begins when you start to notice your own polarity patterns as they arise.

Most leaders don't realize they're stuck until after the tension has escalated. But if you can catch the thinking early—before it becomes behavior—you gain leverage.

Watch for these signs:

- You argue for one side as the "right answer."
- You've stopped asking questions and started defending a position.
- You've "solved" this issue multiple times, but it keeps coming back.
- Different stakeholders have fundamentally opposing views.

In Karina's situation, she began noticing a pattern in her own leadership. "I always lean toward innovation. When efficiency comes up, I feel myself tense up, like it's a bureaucratic attack on creativity."

That awareness changed everything. While innovation was still her preference, she no longer let it drive her automatically.

This connects back to the emotional regulation we explored earlier in the book. When you can catch your instinctive reactions—the tension in your body, the quickening of your thoughts—you create space to respond rather than react.

Your presence changes. And people feel it.

Karina's next step was learning to pause before reacting—to map the tension instead of judging it. That pause became the turning point in how she led through competing priorities.

 TOOL: The Three-Minute Polarity Check

Once you've recognized a polarity, it helps to pause before reacting. Ask yourself four quick questions:

- What's the upside of the view I favor?
- What's the downside of the view I favor?
- What's the upside of the view I resist?
- What's the downside of the view I resist?

Karina tried this with innovation versus efficiency:

- **Innovation** = growth, energy, competitiveness.

  Downside = chaos, rework, lack of focus.

- **Efficiency** = margin, clarity, process improvement.

  Downside = stagnation, inflexibility.

This simple reflection builds your **cognitive flexibility**—the ability to hold opposing truths without collapsing into either-or thinking.

Comfort vs. Challenge

We often talk about creating safe environments as if it means keeping everyone comfortable. But real safety doesn't come from harmony. It comes from honesty—from the strength to hold truth when it's uncomfortable.

This is one of the most overlooked polarities in leadership: the tension between comfort and challenge.

Leaders who lean too heavily on comfort avoid conflict, reach premature consensus, and miss the critical conversations that drive growth. Everything feels smooth...until it doesn't. It's the leadership version of a pothole: The ride is fine until the sudden jolt.

On the other end of the spectrum, leaders who lean too hard on challenge may push too fast, too far. They create pressure without support. Tension rises, but trust breaks.

The goal isn't to hover in the middle—it's to create a place where **candor and care** can coexist. Think of it as a team that can hug it out and then argue productively five minutes later.

That's what creates an environment of trust—not constant agreement, but the confidence that the team can handle the truth.

COACHING CUE: The Comfort Trap

Many leaders chase harmony, thinking it leads to safety. But safety isn't comfort—it's truth-telling.

Psychologically safe teams aren't the most comfortable. They're the ones where people challenge assumptions, surface tension, and take risks without fear of embarrassment.

FIELD NOTE: Signs You May Be in the Comfort Trap

You might be in the comfort trap if:

- Meetings are polite but unchallenging
- There's fast consensus on complex issues
- Problems show up after decisions are made
- Private complaints don't match public dialogue
- There's "agreement"—but little innovation

Comfort without challenge is like a car idling in neutral. The engine's on, but you're going nowhere.

► ELENA: From Harmony to Honesty

Elena, a healthcare executive, led a team that was polite, polished—and paralyzed by avoidance.

"We circled issues without naming them," she told me. "No one wanted to step on toes."

In coaching, she realized she was modeling the very behavior she resented. She said, "I never disagreed publicly. I softened critical feedback. I thought I was protecting the team, but I was really protecting myself."

Her shift began with a moment of productive vulnerability. At the start of a key leadership meeting, she shared a recent mistake, and asked: "What am I missing right now that could help us make better decisions?"

The room froze. Then slowly, her team leaned in. That moment redefined what psychological safety looked like. Not comfort. Not agreement. But truth spoken in a container strong enough to hold it.

MODEL: The Courage Container
Four Practices for Holding Tension Well

Elena's shift points to a broader lesson: real trust is built by leaders who create containers strong enough to hold tension. Here are four practices that help make that real:

1. **Model productive vulnerability.** Share your missteps. Ask for feedback. Make it safe not to be perfect.

2. **Reward challenge, not just agreement.** Thank people publicly for pushback. "That question really helped sharpen our thinking—thank you."

3. **Create rituals of dissent.** Rotate an "official challenger" in key meetings. Use pre-mortems ("What would cause this to fail?") Try "reverse advocacy" where someone argues against their own idea.

4. **Separate ideation from evaluation.** Use green-light and red-light phrases. First brainstorm freely, then critique with structure. Protect divergent thinking before analysis begins.

When leaders practice this, the result is striking. As Elena's team later reflected: "When we were 'nice,' we were distant. Now that we challenge each other, we're actually closer."

As we'll explore further in Chapter 13, this ability to hold tension is a defining mark of executive presence. It's not about appearing flawless or unflappable. It's about embodying the steadiness to stay engaged when there are no easy answers.

READER-TO-LEADER: Your First Mind Flip

Choose one tension you're facing now.

Reflect:

- Am I treating this like a problem to fix or a polarity to navigate?
- Which side do I instinctively lean toward, and why?
- What's valuable in the position I usually resist?
- Where might I be choosing ease over honesty?

Act:

- Use the polarity mapping tool with your team.
- Share one of your biases out loud to model flexibility.
- Next time you hear an uncomfortable truth, pause— then say, "Tell me more about that."

SPIRITUAL CUE: Wisdom Beyond the Binary

Philosopher Ken Wilber teaches: "The more perspectives you can take, the more whole your understanding becomes."

Bashar, as channeled by Darryl Anka, reminds us: "True transformation is not about changing what is. It's about changing your relationship to it."

Polarity thinking is spiritual maturity in action. It requires presence, expansion, and the willingness to hold multiple truths. Not passive, but integrative.

To lead well, you must flip the frame—hold the tension and remain grounded in it.

> **REMEMBER THIS:** *Leadership isn't creating calm. It's creating containers strong enough to hold the storm.*

CROSSING THE THRESHOLD
Stepping in Fully

There comes a moment—sometimes quiet, sometimes jarring—when you realize you are no longer simply doing a job. You are being watched. Your words weigh more. Your moods ripple farther. Your silence speaks volumes. This is the moment leadership becomes less about what you do and more about what you transmit. This is the moment you've crossed the **executive threshold.**

Some leaders resist it, clinging to their old identity as the expert. Others bristle at the scrutiny. But this is the role now. At the executive level, decisions matter—but energy matters more. It's your ability to stabilize a room, the momentum in your body language, the emotional cues you send that either calm or ignite a team. What you bring into the room doesn't stay with you. It spreads.

Let's explore what it means to fully own the executive role as a powerful act of conscious embodiment.

The Mood You Bring Is the Weather They Work In

Chloe had just been promoted to SVP in a global media company when we began coaching. Smart, respected, and warm, she had a loyal team. But with her 360-feedback, a pattern emerged: when Chloe was stressed, the team felt it instantly.

"When she walks in and doesn't say anything, we know something's wrong. It throws off the whole day."

Chloe wasn't yelling. She wasn't visibly upset. But her clipped tone, tight movements, and sighs were being read loudly.

When I reflected this back to her in coaching, she blinked: "I didn't know I had that kind of power."

It turns out, her resting stress face was setting off internal fire alarms.

She did have that kind of power. And so do you. As an executive, your mood becomes the emotional weather system for the team. Whether you mean to or not, you are broadcasting.

You're Not Faking It—You're Embodying It

Malik, a national sales leader in health tech, was smart and had a deeply loyal team. But in senior meetings, his presence fell short. He fidgeted. His tone wandered. His message was unclear.

"I don't want to be fake," he told me when I suggested that he begin thinking of himself as a character he was stepping into.

So we reframed it.

"This isn't about pretending," I said. "At this level, you're not only paid for what you know—you're being paid to embody the role."

We explored how great actors prepare: with intention, emotional congruence, and deep embodiment. Not acting—inhabiting. Malik experimented with posture, pacing, and tone. He practiced stillness before entering the room. At first, it felt awkward—like wearing someone else's shoes—stiff and unfamiliar.

But over time, it molded to him. Then it clicked.

"It's me," he said later. "Just clearer."

That's the shift. Not faking it. Becoming.

The signals you send don't just affect how you're perceived in the moment. Over time, they set the atmosphere your team works in day after day. (We'll go deeper into how leaders shape culture through emotional tone in Chapter 14.)

Every leader leaves an energetic imprint; the best learn to shape it on purpose.

📌 MODEL: Executive Embodiment

The most effective executives don't just manage outcomes. They manage energy. Here's how leadership is communicated, with or without your awareness:

DIMENSION	WHAT IT SIGNALS	WHERE IT SHOWS UP
Energy	Stability, coherence	Mood, nervous system, body language
Voice	Confidence, alignment	Message precision, pace, tone
Optics	Fairness, awareness	Proximity, attention, inclusion
Humanity	Approachability, trust, warmth	Personal story, vulnerability
Follow-through	Integrity, credibility	Action loops, response to feedback

Use this as a lens. You're already communicating these things. The question is: Are you doing it by *default or by design?*

► ERIN: The Optics of Fairness

Erin, a VP at a logistics company, had a long-standing friendship with one of her direct reports, Jake. They'd worked together at a previous company, shared inside jokes, and had informal debriefs over drinks.

Erin didn't see a problem. But the rest of her team did. And they were talking about it:

"Jake always knows what's coming.... He has more access.... His opinion carries more weight."

This wasn't favoritism by design. But optics don't wait for your intent to catch up. In her team's eyes, Jake was playing on home turf while everyone else was stuck in the away locker room.

It was true: Erin was unintentionally signaling preference.

We worked on rebalancing access and visibility, without punishing the friendship. Erin began holding "airtime audits," watching who got the mic and who didn't. She diversified her informal check-ins. And she named her intent out loud: "I'm working on balance. Let me know if I slip."

This transparency built trust—quickly.

Fairness isn't the only optic that shapes how you're read. Visibility does, too. Some leaders vanish behind their work; others reveal so much that their presence starts to drain the room. Either extreme diminishes credibility. Two leaders I coached, Ray and Mira, showed the difference—and what it takes to recalibrate.

► RAY AND MIRA: Calibrating Visibility

Ray, a senior finance manager, was detail-oriented and highly credentialed. His analysis was flawless. But when I ran his 360 interview feedback, one theme emerged: "Ray is sharp, but I don't know him."

He had kept his personal identity hidden. Once a month, he played rhythm guitar in a '90s cover band. Not a single coworker knew. He kept that part of himself far from the office, as if joy and work weren't allowed to mix. Ray believed professionalism required invisibility.

He also had a pattern of asking for feedback, then doing nothing with it. His team noticed. So did his boss. And eventually, despite his talent, Ray stalled out.

Leadership credibility is built on visibility. And it grows when you act on feedback.

Mira, by contrast, was unfiltered. A senior leader in the nonprofit sector, she frequently spoke about her chronic health issues in vivid detail—in meetings, on Slack, in one-on-ones. At first, people responded with care. But over time, they felt depleted.

Her colleagues didn't question her competence. They did question her poor sense of boundaries.

In coaching, we recalibrated how she showed up. She didn't need to stop being open. But she needed to become intentional—saving disclosure for moments that served the relationship or the work, not as a release valve.

You don't need to be robotic. But you do need to be responsible for the impact you leave in the room.

► LINDA AND RAJ: Anchoring Calm in Chaos

Linda, a head of operations, was smart and strategic—and wildly reactive. When things went sideways, she exploded—slamming her pen, raising her voice, snapping at small mistakes.

Her team began hiding bad news.

We worked on slowing her nervous system before meetings, using breath work and a pre-meeting ritual to regulate herself before reacting. Over time, her team began bringing her real issues earlier, not later. Trust followed calm.

Where Linda's reactivity shut down communication, Raj's calm authority opened it up.

Raj, an introverted SVP in retail, did the opposite. During a massive supply chain disruption, he walked into the crisis room, paused, breathed, and said:

"Okay. Let's get our arms around this."

He didn't rush to fill the silence. He let the room breathe. Then he spoke.

Raj didn't just model poise; he made it safe to think clearly. In a room swirling with urgency, his stillness gave others permission to breathe, assess, and act without panic.

This is anchoring: choosing calm as the contagious signal.

Leadership under pressure isn't about flawless control. It's about your poise that steadies others.

As we explored in Chapter 6, energy is a renewable resource when managed with intention. At the executive threshold, it's not just your energy that matters—it's the signal you send. Your composure becomes the anchor others rely on in uncertainty. In a crisis, people don't trust your words until they trust your calm.

TOOL: Rehearsal for the Room

Here's a simple ritual I teach almost every client stepping into higher visibility and high-stakes moments. It only takes thirty seconds and it works.

STEP	WHAT TO DO
Breathe	One deep inhale, one full exhale
Word	Choose one word: Steady. Listen. Guide.
Intention	Set it, e.g., create calm., elevate others, model clarity.
Enter	Use the doorframe as your cue. Leave behind distraction, step into intention.

Like an actor stepping on stage, choose who you want to be *before* the room defines it for you.

Try it for two weeks. After each meeting, rate yourself from 1 to 5—steady, scattered, or somewhere in between. You'll be surprised how fast consistency shows up once you start paying attention.

Even with rituals like this, how you show up isn't fixed. It fluctuates. And sometimes, despite our best intentions, we miss the mark.

When You Realize You've Blown It

We've all had the meeting hangover—the moment you wish you could unsend how you showed up. There's no pill for it. You walk out of a meeting and realize you came across tense, dismissive, scattered, or simply not at your best. You'll feel it in the air—or hear it later in the form of feedback.

Here's the truth: Presence isn't about perfection. It's about recovery.

No matter how intentional you are, you will have moments when your delivery misses the mark. When that happens, the fastest way to rebuild trust is through visible ownership.

Recovery steps

- Name it if needed: A simple acknowledgment can reset the room: "I realize I came across angrier than I intended earlier. Thanks for your patience."

- Reground yourself: Take a breath, calm your system, and reenter with composure.

- Reconnect relationally: A quick human moment—a thank you, a check-in, a question—rebuilds the emotional bridge.

- Course-correct behaviorally: If your rhythm was off, show the shift. Let others feel the reset.

The most trusted executives aren't the ones who never wobble. They're the ones who know how to steady themselves—and the room—when they do.

Mistakes don't ruin presence. Denial, deflection, or defensiveness do.

Under Pressure: The Executive Signal

In high-stakes moments—a board presentation, a crisis call, an emergency town hall—communication isn't just about content. It's about signal management.

What your team or stakeholders remember most isn't the exact words you say. It's how they feel in your presence when you're saying them. In high-stakes moments, scrutiny is magnified. Think of it like airport security: every detail gets inspected, even the things you didn't mean to pack.

That's why even a small move—your breath, your first words, your cadence—can change the tone of the entire room. One client I worked with walked into a crisis call and began with, "Let's take a breath before we start." That ten-second pause changed the tone of the whole conversation.

Key practices for executive communication under fire:

- Anchor yourself before you speak. One breath. One intention. Then begin.
- Lead with structure:

    Situation — What's happening

    Impact — Why it matters

    Action — What we'll do next

- Name emotions without dramatizing them. ("I know this is unsettling. Here's what we're doing.")
- Model poise. Your cadence, eye contact, and tone should transmit confidence and containment.
- Invite questions but don't abdicate authority. Hold space for concerns and move decisions forward.

When stakes rise, people aren't just evaluating what you know. They're scanning for composure, not just strategy.

Calm is contagious. And your calm creates the conditions for clear thinking.

FIELD NOTE: How You Run Meetings is How You Lead

When I mentioned I was writing a leadership book, one of my longtime clients said,

"Please—I'm begging you—put something in about meetings. They're such a waste of time."

He's not wrong. Meetings shape trust, priorities, and energy more than leaders often realize. And if your calendar is stacked back-to-back, you're not leading—you're reacting.

When your days look like a Jenga tower of meetings, you're not building culture. You're just trying not to topple it.

Meetings aren't neutral. Done well, they clarify and connect. Done poorly, they corrode leadership. Before you schedule, accept, or attend one, pause and ask:

- Why are we meeting? Information? Alignment? Decision? If it's not clear, don't go.

- Could this be written instead?

- Who really needs to be in the room? Is this a strategic discussion or theater for it's own sake?

- Are we rewarding insight or airtime? If people are performing participation, the structure is broken.

- Is there a clear owner and next step? If not, you didn't have a meeting; you had aimless airtime.

High-trust leaders know when to decline, send a proxy, or move a discussion into a shared doc.

That's not disengagement. It's discipline.

Try a quick airtime audit: track who speaks, who gets interrupted, and whose ideas move forward. Then act on what you find—rebalance airtime, rotate facilitation, or name the pattern out loud. Meetings reveal more than decisions; they reveal equity, trust, and tone.

This isn't about being anti-meeting. It's choosing to make your time, and your team's time, matter.

Follow-Through Is the Real Meeting

Follow-through is where the personal and the cultural merge. Meetings may create alignment, but it's what you do after that builds trust.

Chantel, a regional VP in tech, began a small practice: after key meetings or one-on-ones, she sent short voice notes to team members: "I heard what you said. I'm following up. You'll hear more from me this week." Fifteen seconds of effort. But the impact was disproportionate. People began saying things like: "I trust her. She follows through. She doesn't just nod; she acts."

Small acts like Chantel's voice notes create emotional continuity, but visible course corrections after moments of friction matter just as much.

Another client, Daniel, a divisional CFO, built trust by practicing what he called "micro course corrections." When a senior peer challenged one of his budgeting assumptions in a meeting, Daniel initially defended his point. But later, after reflection, he realized the other leader had made a valid case.

Instead of ignoring it or pretending it hadn't happened, Daniel sent a short, visible follow-up: "After further review, you're right. I've adjusted our forecast assumptions. Thanks for raising the point." Fifteen seconds of acknowledgment. Zero loss of credibility.

Follow-through doesn't just mean delivering. It means being coachable—and coaching yourself in real time.

READER-TO-LEADER: Owning the Role

Reflect:

* When do I notice my demeanor influencing the room?

- What habits of mine might be sending the wrong message to my team?

- Where might favoritism be creeping in, even if unintentionally?

- What part of me still hesitates to fully step into this role—and what's beneath that?

Act:

- Choose one meeting this week to consciously rehearse how you want to show up.

- Use the Rehearsal for the Room ritual.

- Ask a trusted peer: "What impression do I make when I walk into a room?"

- If you're feeling bold: Ask someone who intimidates you a little.

SPIRITUAL CUE: Energy is Contagious

Ram Dass said it best: "We are all affecting the world every moment, whether we mean to or not."

Stillness transmits. So does tension. And you are the tuning fork for the room.

Rumi invites us to "try not to resist the changes that come your way. Instead, let life live through you."

REMEMBER THIS: *At the executive threshold, everything you transmit echoes wider. When you choose calm, you give others permission to think clearly, act boldly, and trust your lead.*

EMOTIONAL TONE AS LEADERSHIP

Setting the Vibe

As a leader, your tone sets the emotional climate. It doesn't just shape a meeting; it shapes the culture. Tone lingers. It's the atmosphere your people work in day after day—the vibe that outlasts any single conversation.

We've already explored presence and energy, but this is a new dimension.

- Energy is what people feel in your company. It's how you regulate yourself, manage your reserves, and transmit steadiness—or stress—without words.

- Presence is how that energy lands in the moment. It's the attention, gravitas, and intention you bring into a room or a conversation. Presence is the experience others have of you, right now.

- Tone is what endures. It's the emotional backdrop created by your repeated presence over time.

In turbulent times, these three are inseparable. Your energy shapes your presence. Your presence shapes your tone. And your tone shapes your culture.

Tone is also immediate. Long before people interpret your words, they register your pace, your posture, your expression. Psychologist Paul Ekman's work on micro-expressions confirms this: within milliseconds, people pick up on subtle cues—like jaw tension, furrowed brows, fleeting flashes of frustration or doubt. Even a forced smile can transmit pressure.

You may hold your tongue, but your face is still talking.

Scientific Backing: Emotional Contagion and Trust

Organizational psychologists Elaine Hatfield, John Cacioppo, and Richard Rapson describe **emotional contagion**—the way emotion moves through groups almost instantly. Leaders don't just set direction; they set nervous systems. People absorb your stress, calm, hope, or hurry within seconds, often without realizing it.

Jane Dutton's research on **High-Quality Connections (HQC)** shows the same truth from another angle. Even brief moments of what she calls "micro-respect" can elevate trust, performance, and connection. It's not time-consuming. It is tone-defining.

And Stephen M.R. Covey makes the business case plain in *The Speed of Trust*, writing, "Trust is a performance multiplier."

Your culture doesn't run on process. It runs on emotional tone. And that tone starts with you.

Tone Check on the River

My daughter works as a whitewater rafting guide in Colorado, at a company that leads thousands of guests down rivers each season. It's a high-pressure environment: water levels shift daily, equipment must be maintained, rafts have to be organized with the right balance of guides and guests—all while ensuring safety in an often dangerous setting. On top of that, guides are also expected to entertain—to keep people laughing, engaged, and feeling secure even as they face unpredictable rapids. They are simultaneously hosts, coaches, comedians, and guardians.

It's easy to lose your tone in that mix. Guides are giving constant instructions ("How to paddle, how to lean, what to do if you fall out") while scanning for hazards, managing guest fears, and coordinating with one another.

Because they live and work together for months at a time, and understand how quickly tone can change in high pressure periods, they've developed a simple verbal signal. When someone notices any teammate on edge—often the precursor to the whole group catching the same vibe—they gently call out, **"Tone check."** Everyone knows it's a respectful cue to regroup and reset. It's not a critique or a judgment but a moment of self-awareness that benefits the entire team.

I've borrowed this phrase for leaders I coach. Most often, it's a powerful personal reminder to "tone check" before speaking. In some teams, with explicit agreement, it can also become a shared cue. Either way, it shifts attention from stress to steadiness, from reactivity to leadership.

► JESSICA: A Culture Reset From the Top

When Jessica became SVP of Category Strategy at a global food and beverage company, she stepped into a highly visible role with a bruised history. Her predecessor had driven performance through pressure, secrecy, and top-down declarations. On paper, it worked. But morale had cratered. A handful of direct reports had adopted the same style, continuing the legacy of fear, blame, and burnout.

Jessica took a different approach. In her first all-hands

meeting, she said plainly:

"I know this group has been through a lot. I'm not here to gloss over that. I'm here to lead you forward, with clarity, trust, and full accountability."

She backed it up with three concrete moves:

1. Listening sessions where people could speak candidly (anonymously, if preferred)

2. Transparent decision frameworks that explained the *why* behind changes

3. Firm follow-through on accountability gaps

One senior leader, Evan, was a holdover from the previous regime. Charismatic but caustic, he lobbied loudly for promotion while offloading work and undermining Jessica behind closed doors. She coached him directly, set clear expectations, and gave him multiple chances. After three months, no change. She let him go.

"The air shifted immediately," one director said. "We realized she meant what she said—and we mattered."

Jessica didn't change culture with slogans. She changed it with tone. Steady, consistent, and visible.

► ASHLEY: Building a Culture of Connection

If Jessica reset the frequency from the top, Ashley rebuilt it from the ground up.

Promoted to lead public-facing staff across a regional bank's branches, Ashley inherited a team worn down by turnover, pandemic stress, and top-down directives that changed week to week.

Her first few weeks were quiet. Too quiet. People averted eye contact. Conversations stayed surface-level. The frontline didn't yet trust she was really *with* them.

So she began a simple ritual: morning touchpoints. Short team huddles that began not with updates, but with breath work.

"Let's take one deep breath in...and out. What energy are you bringing today?"

At first, it felt awkward. Then it became grounding.

She added:

- Casual branch walk-throughs where she made eye contact, used names, and asked real questions

- A "Name & Story" board in the breakroom with photos and passions

- Short, handwritten thank-you notes, left in mail slots

Ashley didn't overhaul organizational structure. She shifted the tone—creating small, human cues of connection. And in doing so, she gave her team the room to reconnect.

► JONAS: When Calm Feels Like Absence

If Jessica led with clarity and Ashley with connection, Jonas led with absence.

As managing director of a global executive search firm, Jonas had built a powerhouse reputation advising Fortune 100 companies on leadership pipelines and cultural fit, and executive presence. But inside his own firm, his own presence was unraveling. He rarely led team meetings. His check-ins were infrequent. His tone was polite but distant.

"They know what I expect," he said in coaching. "I've hired great people. I trust them."

But trust wasn't what his team felt. What they felt was a vacuum.

"He doesn't correct us—but he doesn't see us either," said one team member. "I feel like I'm performing into a void," said another.

Jonas wasn't broadcasting stress or judgment. Actually, he wasn't broadcasting anything. And in that void, the culture drifted.

We worked on what I call **gentle broadcasting**: simple cues that signal presence without overexertion—naming what's working, reiterating priorities, and restating values with warmth.

Jonas didn't need to be louder. He needed to be deliberate. Once he began showing up—visibly, emotionally, energetically—the team recalibrated quickly.

FIELD NOTE: Small Signals, Big impact

Brad was one of my neighbors, and led the biggest customer account at a global consumer products company. Every Friday, he took one team member out to lunch on his own dime. "No work talk," he'd say. "I just want to get to know you."

His team adored him. Why? He noticed them. He valued them. And he showed up for them—in simple, deliberate ways.

The fact that the lunches weren't expensed mattered too. It signaled a generosity of spirit because he chose to care. "Lunch with Brad" became a tradition everyone looked forward to. You'd hear teammates say, "It's your week for lunch with Brad? Lucky you!"

This wasn't fluff. It was tone, made tangible.

MODEL: The Three Frequencies of Culture

Every leader broadcasts energy, but over time those signals settle into a prevailing tone—what people reliably expect to feel from you. That's our cultural frequency.

Each frequency creates a distinct vibe, and people can sense it intuitively.

FREQUENCY	VIBE	COMMON PHRASES
Control	Tension	"Just get it done." • "Who's accountable?" • "Why didn't I know?" • "That's not what I asked for." • "Run this by me first." • "This shouldn't have happened."
Connection	Belonging	"Tell me more." • "I appreciate you naming that." • "How are you doing?" • "That insight stuck with me." • "What do you need from me?" • "We'll figure it out together."
Clarity	Focus	"Here's the why." • "Let's connect this to the big picture." • "What does success look like?" • "Let's simplify." • "We're not changing direction; we're evolving the plan."

You don't need to live in one frequency. But when culture feels wobbly, it helps to ask: What am I transmitting now—and what's needed here?

The behaviors below are subtle, but powerful. They either build cultural trust or quietly undermine it.

BEHAVIOR	TRUST BUILDER	TRUST ERODER
Emotional tone	Calm, grounded energy	Stress, reactivity, tension
Communication	Clear, timely, transparent	Vague, delayed, inconsistent
Recognition	Frequent, specific, inclusive	Rare, generic, or uneven
Presence	Attentive, warm, values-aligned	Distracted, aloof, performative
Follow-through	Reliable and visible	Silent or inconsistent

You can't shift cultural frequency if you're transmitting static. Even one deep exhale, a posture reset, or a mental reframe before walking into a room can change the entire tone you send.

Trust isn't built in big speeches. It's built in the small moments where your tone matches your intent.

COACHING INSIGHT: Generational Comfort Zones

Tone doesn't show up the same way for every generation. Younger professionals—especially Gen Z—often feel more fluent expressing emotion digitally than face-to-face. But what feels natural online can feel exposed or even performative in the room.

This isn't a lack of depth; it's a difference in expression.

If you're a rising leader:

- Notice when you avoid emotional engagement.
- Try real-time check-ins, not just emojis or Slack replies.
- Practice staying present when conversations get uncomfortable.

If you're leading across generations:

- Don't mistake quiet for disengagement.
- Support presence over polish—especially when trust is still forming.
- Offer grace as people practice new ways of showing up.

Connection grows with practice, not age.

Presence Without Proximity

Managing your leadership signal is more complex when you lose proximity. In remote and hybrid leadership, presence must reach across spaces without losing force.

Hybrid leadership raises the stakes. You're not influencing people just through what you say but through what they feel in the gaps between Zoom calls, Slack replies, and time zones.

The challenge isn't just being seen. It's making others feel seen when you're not in the room.

As you rise, your impact needs to expand, without dilution. You're influencing more people, across more settings and dynamics—some of which you'll never see directly. Yet what you transmit still matters. Perhaps more than ever.

You're not just maintaining credibility on-screen. You're shaping trust and culture across distance, difference, and delay. Face-to-face, you may have minutes to convey nuance through tone and body language. Online, where attention is fleeting, you may only have seconds.

Presence without proximity is the new leadership skill.

Ask yourself:

- Do I extend presence across time zones, not just during my own work hours?
- Do I build relationships beyond transactional meetings?
- Do I recognize unseen effort?
- Do I convey steadiness through both screen and silence?

As AI automates more functional tasks, emotional tone becomes one of the few signals leaders still fully own. Algorithms can schedule updates, but they can't rebuild trust after silence. They can't sense when someone is withdrawing—or restore connection with genuine attention. That's still yours to lead.

► KRISTIN: Stretching Across Distance

Kristin, a Vice President based in Dallas, led a complex technical operations team scattered across two continents. Early in her role, she discovered something unsettling: Her India-based team often felt peripheral, not intentionally excluded but sidelined by US-centered rhythms.

It wasn't about time zones. It was about visibility.

She realized that despite her best intentions, the team's experience was shaped by a thousand small cues, such as who got the "prime" meeting times, who had real-time access to her, or whose wins were celebrated out loud.

Kristin made small but strategic changes. She:

- Rotated meeting times quarterly so no one always bore the scheduling burden.

- Created asynchronous "wins channels" where successes could be seen and celebrated by everyone.

- Launched quarterly global town halls, inviting pre-submitted questions to level the playing field across language and bandwidth differences.

Within six months, something shifted. Engagement scores rose. Participation deepened. People started speaking up more.

Not because Kristin worked 24/7.

But because her leadership began to stretch—intentionally—across space and difference, without exhausting her.

She didn't just show up on camera. She built trust. People felt seen, valued, and included, wherever they were.

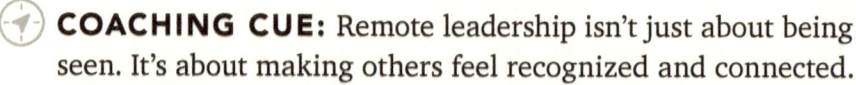 **COACHING CUE:** Remote leadership isn't just about being seen. It's about making others feel recognized and connected.

FIELD NOTE: Habits That Build Trust Across Distance

HABIT	CULTURAL SIGNAL
Consistent camera use and engagement	"I'm present, even from afar."
Intentional pre-meeting small talk	"You matter beyond the agenda."
Clear, structured meetings with tone checks	"I sense the room—even virtually."
Recognition of unseen efforts	"I see beyond the output."
Calm escalation practices (no panic pings)	"We handle challenge without panic."
Time zone inclusive rituals (such as asynchronous wins)	"Everyone belongs to the mission, not just to the clock."
Separate connection time from project time	"We nurture connection, not just output."

 READER-TO-LEADER: Leading by Tone and Trust.

Reflect:

- What is my default tone at work—calm, rushed, warm, distracted?

- What messages do I send through pace, body language, and response?

- How do I handle bad news—do I invite honesty or make people hesitate?

- Are my values visible in daily interactions or only in slides and slogans?

- Do skip-level employees feel at ease around me?

- Are people sharing ideas—or just reporting updates?

Act:

- Choose one meeting to enter with clear intention.

- Recognize unseen effort—something that might otherwise go unnoticed.

- Ask a trusted colleague: "What's it like to be in my presence when I'm under pressure?" Then listen without defending.

- Close one interaction with warmth, focus, or appreciation—and notice what shifts.

- Create your own small, repeatable signal (like "Coffee with [Your Name]" or a weekly drop-in) to build trust through consistent, human connection.

Spiritual Cue: Be the Calm in the Storm

The energy you broadcast lingers longer than most people realize. And sometimes, the most grounded person in the room resets the tone for everyone else.

The most impactful leaders don't just manage tasks—they manage tone.

As Rumi reminds us: "Before you speak, let your words pass through three gates: Is it true? Is it necessary? Is it kind?" This doesn't mean filtering yourself into passivity. Rather, choose your energy with care, especially when others feel overwhelmed.

Spiritual teacher Tara Brach puts it beautifully: "The quality of your presence is the first gift you give." You don't have to be perfect. But your grounded presence might be the permission someone else needs to exhale.

That's leadership by tone. It's transmitted not by force, but by the atmosphere you create.

REMEMBER THIS: *Your tone is the culture your people feel first. Set it with care.*

WHEN THE CLIMB STALLS

Resetting Identity

Leadership is not just a title. It's how you show up when the path disappears beneath you. Whether it's the best of times or the worst of times, great leaders rise to the occasion.

Every leader I've worked with—regardless of industry, tenure, or level—eventually hits a moment they didn't plan for. It might be a rupture, a reckoning, a pause that wasn't voluntary, or a plan that fell apart. Sometimes it's personal. Sometimes it's professional. But it's always disorienting.

Maybe it's the aging parent who suddenly needs full-time care. The layoff that came without warning. The reorganization that erased your influence overnight. The new boss who does not value your contributions. Or maybe it's the promotion that never came, even though you'd done everything right.

Sometimes, it kicks you off the mountain you spent years climbing.

This chapter is here to name those moments—and the identity crisis they often trigger—so that you can navigate disruption with clarity and resilience, then plan what comes next.

The Elephant in the Room

In almost every coaching engagement, at some point, the **real** conversation begins. It's not about org charts, performance metrics, or strategy decks. It's about life—the things leaders rarely say out loud.

It might be the chronically ill child. The panic attacks. The partner who resents your long hours. The parent who no longer recognizes you.

None of these show up on a résumé, but these pressures shape leadership more than any development plan ever will. The cost of keeping up appearances while carrying private burdens is staggering.

One client, Carla, held a demanding, well-paid leadership role in a fast-moving corporate culture. She was praised for her responsiveness and commitment. But she had missed her daughter's birthday three years in a row. "They get my best hours," she said quietly. "My family gets the leftovers."

She wasn't being dramatic. She was telling the truth.

Many companies talk a good game about flexibility: unlimited PTO, mental health days, 'family-first" values. But the reality is often very different. Work-life balance? It's more like work-money balance.

The unspoken contract is this: You will be well-paid, but we own your time. Unless leaders name that tradeoff and make conscious choices, the job will take everything they offer—and ask for more.

Identity Shock

When leadership is working, it feels powerful. You're trusted. You're needed. You're seen. But there's a hidden cost: the more successful you become, the more likely you are to overidentify with your role. You likely see yourself as respected, hardworking, and responsible:

"I'm the high-potential one."

"I'm the face of this program."

"I'm the one who always delivers."

And then something happens. The organization is restructured. A new leader comes in. Your team is cut. Or technology disrupts everything you built.

That's what happened to Eli, a rising star in the tech division of a major retailer. Strategic, steady, and admired, he was considered untouchable—until AI innovation swept through his department. His role, and his entire team, were eliminated. Eli wasn't just grieving a job. He was grieving the identity he'd worked so hard to build.

That's identity shock.

Sometimes derailment isn't about performance at all. It's about a political, cultural, or strategic shift that reclassifies your presence as inconvenient.

Anika had been promoted to lead DEI initiatives at a large company in 2020. She brought energy, credibility, and strong cross-functional influence. She was weeks away from being named Chief Diversity Officer.

And then the climate changed. Not just inside the company. Outside it. DEI became politicized, demonized, and divisive. New pressures emerged. Suddenly, meetings were canceled. The wins were downplayed. Her leadership was quietly erased.

She was told, "It's just a shift in priorities." But it wasn't *just* a shift. It was a takedown.

In coaching she said, "They made me believe I was the future. And then they acted like I was the problem. And I almost believed them."

The system didn't fail Anika because she wasn't excellent. It failed her because it couldn't hold what it once celebrated.

When Disruption Hits

The ground can shift beneath you even when you've done every-thing right. Careers can stall, not because of what you did but because of forces far outside your control. I see this more and more these days across every sector—leaders blindsided not by performance gaps but by volatility they couldn't predict.

A sudden recession, a spike in interest rates, or market panic can erase entire divisions overnight. Political or regulatory upheavals—a new law, tariff war, or geopolitical conflict—can undo years of progress. Technology can render a function obso-lete in a matter of months. Pandemics, climate disasters, or supply chain collapse can ripple across industries without warning. Even boardroom power plays—coups, hostile takeovers, abrupt leader-ship changes—can destabilize careers that once felt secure.

And just as often, the derailers come from private life. A chronic health condition. A mental health struggle. Divorce. Caregiving. Financial loss. Identity theft. The ache of estrange-ment or isolation.

These disruptions don't just slow a career; they can unseat it. When this happens, I often see leaders fall into familiar but unhelpful patterns:

- Shock and denial: "I'll just push through."
- Overwork: taking on more to prove worth.
- Withdrawal: pulling back from colleagues or mentors.
- Hypercontrol: micromanaging as a way to manage fear.
- Emotional volatility: mood swings, overreactions, second-guessing.
- Blaming and scapegoating: looking outward instead of inward.
- Self-doubt and identity crisis: "Maybe I was never cut out for this."

What's most damaging isn't the disruption. It's believing you should be able to handle it alone, or that the same old tools will work in a completely new reality. Left unchecked, these patterns are like spinning your wheels in mud: lots of effort, no forward motion.

Coaching Through Disruption: How to Rebuild

When disruption hits—whether it's a layoff, a divorce, a reorganization, or burnout—most leaders instinctively try to power through. But disruption isn't a productivity problem. It's an identity recalibration.

This is where the real coaching begins. Not in fixing the external, but in steadying the internal. Here are the strategies that reset leaders most effectively in those moments.

Normalize the Experience

"This isn't supposed to happen to someone like me." That's often the first sentence I hear. It's gutting to watch a strong, accomplished leader unravel silently. Sleeplessness. Shame. Compulsive overwork. Numbness. From the outside, they're functioning. Inside, they're falling apart.

High achievers often believe setbacks are a sign of personal failure—when they're really a normal part of any leadership arc. Even exceptional leaders stall. Even the most talented professionals get passed over, laid off, restructured, or burned out.

You are not broken. You are being reshaped.

As a coach, I often share anonymized examples of clients who went through similar moments and emerged wiser, healthier, and more aligned. Not to minimize the pain but to break the illusion that success equals immunity.

The faster you can say, "This is the way it is," the faster you can get your power back.

The Sphere-of-Control Framework

When everything feels out of control, your brain will scramble for something to hold onto. That's when people start over-functioning—taking on more than their share, micromanaging, or spiraling into anxiety.

Here's the reset: Draw three concentric circles on a page.

- In the center ring: Write what you can control—your schedule, your self-talk, your habits.

- In the middle ring: Write what you can influence—team morale, peer alignment, project direction.

- In the outer ring: Write what you cannot control—market conditions, other people's choices, the reorganization, the economy.

Now list everything on your mind, and place each item in the right ring. Then, ask yourself: What energy am I wasting on the outer ring, those things I can't control? What would shift if I redirected that energy toward what I can actually control?

This quick visual exercise calms the overwhelm and restores focus in minutes.

Preserve Your Core Identity

When the climb stalls, many leaders think they need to reinvent themselves entirely. That's rarely true. More often, they need to carry their strengths forward in a new way.

Start by naming your core leadership strengths—the throughlines that have been true across every role you've had. Strategic thinking? Calm under pressure? Translating complexity into clarity?

Then ask yourself: How can I express those same strengths differently in this new reality, without abandoning who I am?

This simple shift matters. It prevents the all-or-nothing

thinking that leads to rash career moves or identity collapse. It reminds you: "I am still me. My role has changed, but my value hasn't disappeared."

If you're in the middle of disruption, it can feel like you're in fog. This is where I often reach for simple models for clients to give shape to what otherwise feels messy. Two of my favorites are Bridges and GROW.

The Bridges Transition Model

Developed by William Bridges, this model reframes change not as a single moment but as a three-stage emotional journey. This model works because it names what leaders are already living through:

1. **Endings:** What is truly ending? What are you losing? What must be grieved?

2. **The Neutral Zone:** The in-between space. You're not who you were, and not yet who you're becoming. It feels slow, messy, and uncertain—and that's normal.

3. **New Beginnings:** The stage where things start to click— new clarity, new direction, new possibilities.

Leaders often try to rush to a new beginning without honoring the ending. That never works. Naming the ending matters. So does allowing yourself to linger in the neutral zone without calling it failure. Sometimes moving through the fog is the work.

The GROW Model, Disruption Edition

This familiar goal-setting model becomes even more powerful when applied to identity disruption. This helps leaders shift from spinning to steadying, because it's not a five-year plan—it's just one honest step forward.

Here's how the model shifts in moments of disruption.

- G—Goal

  What is meaningful and achievable now, not before every-thing changed, but **now**? Don't force old goals into a new reality.

- R—Reality

  What's true? Not just externally but internally. What are you feeling, fearing, avoiding? This is where self-honesty matters most.

- O—Options

  What haven't you considered yet? Who could you talk to? What would you try if fear weren't running the show?

- W—Way Forward

  What small step can you take this week? Don't overthink it. Action creates clarity.

The GROW Model gives you a foothold when your path feels stuck—and sometimes that's enough to start moving forward again.

Retirement Shock and What's Next

Some leaders aren't disrupted by a crisis at all—they simply retire. And that can be its own identity shock.

I've seen too many high achievers enter retirement with nothing more than a vague plan to "relax." Within months, they feel aimless. Some decline. Others fall into passive routines, drink too much, or disappear from their own lives.

Why? Because they never developed a vision for themselves beyond the role. This identity vacuum has a name: **Retirement Syndrome**—a mix of helplessness, loss of meaning, and a creep-ing sense of being irrelevant. Retirement clears your calendar, but it can also destabilize your nervous system.

The statistics are sobering. Long-term public-health studies have found that the risk of heart attack or stroke jumps by nearly

40% in the first year after retirement—a physiological echo of how hard sudden loss of purpose hits the body. Researchers call this the "retirement shock window"—a period when structure, social connection, and purpose drop off abruptly, and the body responds with elevated stress.

Harvard researchers have found a similar pattern on the emotional side: many high performers experience a sharp decline in well-being during this same window, not because they miss the meetings or deadlines but because they lose the identity those things once anchored.

What's missing isn't busyness. It's alignment. A gym membership won't fix the ache of irrelevance. A bucket list won't create identity—unless, of course, you plan to become an Instagram travel influencer.

The antidote? Vital engagement. The leaders who thrive after a career are those who reframe retirement as a new era of contribution and conscious impact.

▶ MIKE: Redefining Retirement as a Legacy Move

This one's personal. Mike, my husband, spent his career as an attorney and general counsel at one of the world's largest retailers. For decades, his calendar was packed, his responsibilities weighty, and his identity tightly woven into corporate life.

But when that chapter ended, he didn't plan to slow down. He planned to reinvest—his time, his energy, and his purpose. "Retirement isn't a finish line," he once said to me. "It's a reallocation of energy."

Mike asked himself three questions before stepping away:

1. Do I actually want to retire? (Not everyone does. Some people want more choice, not less work.)

2. Can I afford to retire? (Not just comfortably, but securely—without trading freedom for anxiety.)

3. What will I do with forty to sixty hours a week, every week? (That's where most people stumble. Beyond sleep and travel plans, what will give your days shape?)

Mike didn't stop leading. He shifted how he led. He trained for endurance events to stay vital and engaged, and he launched a nonprofit that now supports dozens of outdoor experiences each year for people ages two to seventy-five.

Watching him create this next chapter has reshaped my view of leadership transitions. He didn't just retire. He redefined what contribution looks like—on his own terms.

And here's the takeaway: Mike's story is one example of what's possible. You don't need triathlons or nonprofits to thrive post-career. But you do need intentional purpose.

You don't age out of purpose. You grow into it.

SPIRITUAL CUE: Transition as Sacred

As Paul Selig's guides often teach: "You cannot be who you were and become who you are."

Transitions, especially those that involve the loss of a role, are not just logistical. They are energetic thresholds.

The channeled wisdom of Abraham Hicks reminds us that we are always in a state of becoming. And the Z's, channeled through Lee Harris, frame retirement not as an ending but as an opening—the most liberated expression of your soul's values.

The role may change. But your essence still has work to do.

Ask: What if this next chapter isn't a winding down but a rising up? Or both?

Want to Retire Well? Start Now!

A word from your coach: If you're within five to ten years of retirement and haven't thought seriously about what life looks like beyond your title, start now. I've seen too many high performers walk away with plenty of money but no plan for meaning. They thought they'd travel, sleep in, "enjoy life." And within a few months, they felt restless and disconnected.

You need more than a financial glide path. You need a *purpose glide path*. Start designing it while you still have the network, energy, and influence to shape what comes next.

 ## TOOL: Designing Your Retirement Glide Path

The best retirement transitions don't happen overnight. They happen with intention over time. A glide path allows you to preserve identity, explore new rhythms, and exit on your own terms.

Five ways to design one that works for you:

- Start the glide early. Don't wait until your exit is announced. Begin phasing down responsibilities, handing off key functions, and creating space to experiment with what's next.

- Run retirement rehearsals. Use long vacations or sabbaticals to simulate unstructured time. Pay attention to how you feel when the calendar isn't full. What energizes you? What drains you?

- Reframe what retirement means. It's not an ending; it's an evolution. From title to legacy. From operator to mentor. From public identity to personal alignment.

- Acknowledge the resistance. Many leaders don't fear irrelevance. They fear stillness. Name that. Wanting structure, contribution, and purpose doesn't mean you're failing at retirement.

- Create meaning before you need it. Don't wait until you exit to build friendships, hobbies, or service roles. Start now. Meaning is easier to carry forward when it's already woven into your life.

READER-TO-LEADER: Redefining Success, on Your Terms

If this chapter stirred uncertainty, regret, or possibility, don't rush to fix it. Sit with it. Then start here:

Reflect:

- What part of your identity have you tied to your job, title, or company?

- Have you ever experienced a disruption that made you question who you are?

- If your climb paused today, what would you regret having postponed?

Act:

- Use the Bridges Model to identify where you are in the transition.

- Sketch your Sphere of Control this week and act from clarity.

- Start designing your personal glide path—what will your new life look like in rhythm, energy, and purpose?

> **REMEMBER THIS:** *Leadership doesn't end when the climb pauses. Sometimes, that's where it begins.*

THE LONG VIEW

Living Your Legacy

"Your legacy is every life you've touched." —Maya Angelou

Legacy doesn't begin with your retirement party or that heartfelt LinkedIn farewell. It begins now—in how you show up, how people feel in your presence, and what they learn, intentionally or not, by watching how you lead.

Some leaders define success by what they achieve. Others define it by what they enable. Legacy lives in the echo of your example.

Most people think of legacy as what lingers—how you shape others, what they carry forward, the imprint that remains when you're gone. And that's true. But legacy also shows up in quieter pivots: in how you reorient your leadership, reclaim your confidence, or steady a culture when it drifts.

Let's begin with Alan.

► **ALAN: From Achiever to Builder**

Sometimes what looks like burnout is growth trying to happen.

That was the case for Alan, a highly respected CEO of a mid-size manufacturing company. A former operations leader turned turnaround specialist, Alan had built a two-decade career focused on efficiency, results, and scale. He'd earned the titles, the accolades, and the financial rewards. By all external measures, he had won the game.

But when we began working together, Alan was restless. "I've hit every target I ever aimed for. But I'm not excited anymore. And I don't know what to do with that."

Alan wasn't burned out in the classic sense. He was on a plateau—the kind that doesn't look like failure but feels like it. He still performed, but without joy. He still made decisions, but with less imagination. The drive that once fueled him now fell flat.

What he described as "hitting a wall" was really something else. He wasn't depleted. He was evolving.[5]

We mapped the chapters of his career and the drivers in each, clarified his current values, which had quietly shifted toward mentorship, wisdom-sharing, and service—and used future-self visualization to reconnect him with a bigger purpose. What emerged was a realization: what once lit him up (recognition, scale, problem-solving) no longer held meaning. But something else was waiting underneath.

Alan redefined success not as doing more, but as building what's next. He began coaching emerging leaders and seeded a sustainability initiative—not for the ROI, but because it was right. He said yes to industry speaking engagements where he talked about failures, not wins. He focused on preparing future leaders, seeing it not as a formality but as one of his most

---

5 See also Chapter 6, "The Energy Shift," where we explored how what feels like depletion may actually be a sign of transition, not failure.

important contributions. And he championed a workforce training initiative for underserved communities. He also came to see succession as one of his greatest responsibilities.

It wasn't a reinvention. But it was a reorientation—from scale to meaning and from delivery to legacy. Within a year, Alan's tone began to change the culture. His senior team reported more trust and steadiness. Younger managers said they felt seen, not sized up. He hadn't stopped driving results—he'd stopped driving himself. What changed wasn't his output, but his peace.

Eighteen months later, even his board noticed the difference. They described him as calmer, sharper, and more connected to purpose than they'd ever seen. And Alan himself reclaimed the sense of drive that had gone missing. "I spent twenty years climbing the mountain," he said. "Now I want to help others find their path up—and leave the mountain better than I found it."

That's the legacy pivot, a shift toward what will matter long after you're gone.

Alan's story shows how legacy can emerge when achievement matures into contribution. But legacy isn't only about pivoting while still at your peak. Sometimes it's about reclaiming your voice after it's been silenced. That was the case for Thomas.

► THOMAS: From Burned Out to Beacon

Thomas was a seasoned hand in health care. He had once held C-suite titles: COO and President of Hospitals. Now, in his mid-50s, he was stepping into a Director of Compliance role at a regional health system. To some, it looked like a step back. But for his CEO, it was strategic. He saw Thomas as a stabilizing presence, someone who could anchor the leadership team with wisdom and experience.

But that anchor didn't drop. Thomas showed up hesitant, soft-spoken, and almost invisible in senior meetings. His CEO, still hopeful, encouraged him to work with a coach.

In our first session, Thomas shared the real story: "I used to speak up, until it cost me. A board chair once undermined me in public. I stopped raising my hand after that."

He wasn't lacking in ideas. But he was still carrying the scars for expressing them. Many leaders carry this same hesitation. Once you've been cut down in public, it's hard to risk raising your hand again.

We worked on reframing his role, not as a retreat but as a return. This wasn't the epilogue of his career. It was a chance to shape culture from a different position of power.

Once Thomas tapped into that lens, everything shifted. He started mentoring junior leaders. He began offering quiet but incisive insight during strategy meetings. He ran calm, clear debriefs after tense stakeholder calls.

His CEO later told me, "He's the ballast. He's not loud but he's trusted. And that steadies the whole ship."

Thomas didn't need a new title. He needed a new narrative. And that became his legacy.

Thomas's story shows how legacy can be reclaimed—how a leader can steady culture by returning to presence after a period of silence. But legacy also shows up as reinvention: shifting your whole style of influence. That was the case for Darius.

► DARIUS: From Driver to Oracle

Darius had built his leadership brand through control. A field operations lead for a global cruise line, he was known for precision, intensity, and results.

When he was promoted to enterprise strategy, everything changed. Now his job was to influence across silos. To listen more than speak. To trade authority for alignment.

He floundered. "I'm used to solving problems. Here, I'm just floating. Am I even adding value?" he would ask colleagues. In coaching, he often returned to one question: "What am I here for if I'm not the expert anymore?"

We talked about energetic presence. About shifting from driver to guide. Slowly, he started listening more and saying less. He shared stories with context instead of barking answers. He joined onboarding sessions and told younger employees what no one had told him: "The pressure never disappears, but your presence can change how it's felt." It was striking to hear him use that word. Presence wasn't abstract. It was real, and his team could feel it.

Months later, after a particularly messy cross-functional meeting, a peer turned to him and said, "You didn't take over. But you made it easier for us to think clearly."

That was the moment Darius became the compass, not the commander. Darius had discovered what we described in Chapter 8: real gravitas isn't about commanding attention. It's about shifting energy.

FIELD NOTE: From Control to Guidance

Here's how this shift from control to guidance often plays out in the energy leaders transmit and the behaviors people experience:

FROM...	TO
Doing	Guiding
Solving	Coaching
Protecting	Empowering
Leading meetings	Shaping conversations
Commanding	Cultivating

This is what presence looks like in motion. It's less about directing every outcome and more about creating conditions where others can grow.

Legacy doesn't just live in your own evolution. It shows up in how others remember you. Sometimes, it's the imprint of a single leader's style, for better or worse.

► SARAH AND MIKE: The Tale of Two Legacies

Early in my finance career, I worked for a large Wall Street bank and reported to a VP named Sarah. Each morning, I arrived hopeful, eager to learn, contribute, and grow. But within the first hour, that hope would unravel.

Sarah kept everything to herself. Even though we sat on the same open floor, she offered minimal interaction. Most of her time was spent in meetings I wasn't invited to. When we traveled together to visit client companies, it should have been a golden development opportunity. But she remained aloof, offering only crumbs of guidance.

It was demoralizing. After six months of this silent treatment, I mustered the nerve to ask her SVP for a transfer. He agreed, and I landed in a new team with a leader named Mike—Sarah's polar opposite.

Mike was generous with his time and inclusive in his leadership, and he created a warm, collaborative culture. He hosted team lunches, made space for learning moments, and treated each of us like we mattered. Turns out a free lunch sometime says more than strategy memos.

Within a year, Mike was poached by another major bank—and nearly his entire team jumped with him. Sarah, meanwhile, was quietly reassigned to a smaller region. Her legacy had spoken for itself.

As Frances Frei and Anne Morriss write in *Harvard Business Review*, trust grows when people feel understood (empathy), when they believe your reasoning is sound, and when they see your values lived out consistently. Mike's success wasn't just tactical. It was relational. His legacy wasn't his title—it was the way he led.

Mentorship as a Living Legacy

Legacy doesn't start with retirement speeches. It starts with how you coach your team now. It's built into the stories you tell, the belief you extend, the stretch assignments you protect.

Great legacy leaders:

- Mentor both direct reports and adjacent rising stars.
- Share stories of failure and learning, not just wins.
- Offer air cover for bold experiments.
- Create space for voices that don't often get the mic.
- Make time for those conversations that aren't on the meeting agenda.

These aren't extra tasks. They're the very fabric of how legacy gets woven into daily leadership.

Mentorship is not about cloning yourself. It's about shaping conditions for growth that outlive your tenure.

FIELD NOTE: The Legacy Loop—Reverse Mentoring

One of the most powerful ways to live your legacy is to let someone junior teach you. It's called **reverse mentoring**, and it keeps you honest, current, and human.

Younger colleagues have taught my clients why meme culture is emotional shorthand, and how feedback lands differently by generation. I've seen senior leaders rethink team communication after a junior colleague explained neurodiversity and how different brains process information. In one global firm, reverse mentoring even reshaped recruiting strategy when early-career hires shared how interview questions landed across cultures.

The point isn't to become fluent in TikTok or jargon overnight. The point is to stay curious enough to ask, to listen, and to let yourself be shaped by those coming up behind you. Reverse mentoring isn't a novelty—it's a feedback loop that keeps organizations alive. When senior leaders stay curious enough to be taught, they model adaptability, and that becomes contagious. Reverse mentoring doesn't just help keep you current. It shows your team that you're still learning, and that humility may be the most enduring part of your legacy.

Legacy isn't only visible in titles or formal recognition. It lives in the small echoes of daily leadership—the phrases people repeat, the habits they carry forward, the stories they tell about you when you're not in the room. One nonprofit client once told me, "I'll never have a building named after me. But I know I helped three women become directors, and they're each helping five more." She wasn't chasing headlines. She was creating quiet momentum.

► MARK'S LEGACY: No Title Required

Mark was an executive assistant to a series of senior leaders. He didn't manage a team. He didn't make decisions in boardrooms. But he was the steady pulse of the department.

He welcomed new hires with handwritten notes. Remembered birthdays without a calendar reminder. Noticed when someone was having a hard week, and quietly made sure they weren't alone. He was the glue that held the team together, without ever asking for recognition.

But when he left the company, the feel of the place changed, and not in a way anyone could easily name. People across departments said the same thing: "It doesn't feel the same without him."

When a new leader arrived, they said: "I keep hearing about this Mark. What was his role?"

The answer: "He was the one who made this place feel like it mattered."

Mark didn't leave behind a strategic plan. He left behind a way of being. That was his legacy.

SPIRITUAL CUE: The Legacy of We

Many Indigenous traditions teach the principle of considering how today's decisions will affect the next seven generations. This wisdom reminds us that true leadership transcends immediate results.

Robin Wall Kimmerer, writing from her Potawatomi Native American tradition, frames leadership as a form of sacred reciprocity—not just taking from the system but giving back more than you receive.

This reminds me of a truth I came to love during the six years my family and I lived in Africa: the spirit of Ubuntu—"I am because we are." It's a way of seeing the world, centered on belonging, responsibility, and mutual uplift.

Legacy, in this light, is never solo. It's shared, passed down, and collective. As the African proverb teaches: "If you want to go fast, go alone. If you want to go far, go together."

Legacy doesn't begin at retirement. It begins now—in the ripples of generosity, strength, and belief you pass to others.

READER-TO-LEADER: The Long View

Reflect:

- If your leadership were a story, what chapter are you in?
- What kind of echo—or imprint—are you creating?

Act:

- Identify two to three people in your organization you could begin mentoring. Reach out to one this week.

- Think of someone junior to you who inspires you. Invite them to teach you something.

- Notice one habit you model every day. Ask yourself: is this the echo I want to leave?

> **REMEMBER THIS:** *You don't need a platform to shape culture. You just need presence, intention, and the courage to care.*

THE TORCH YOU CARRY

Leadership That Lasts

If you've made it here, you're not just interested in becoming a better leader—you're committed. And that commitment is rare.

Over the years, I've seen leaders at every stage of the journey—some beginning with raw ambition, some weathering disruption, others wrestling with legacy. The ones who endure, the ones who shape cultures and lives for the better, are the ones who learn to carry the torch.

The torch is presence. It's steadiness when others falter. It's light in a room that feels uncertain. And it's not a prize you win—it's a responsibility you accept.

Some leaders keep their torch to themselves. Others pass it generously, igniting confidence, clarity, and courage in those around them. That, to me, is lasting leadership.

Integration: Tying It All Together

Leadership presence isn't a single breakthrough moment. It's an ongoing calibration over time through feedback, tension, trust, and practice. The stories, models, and tools you've explored are not the finish line. They are your invitation to begin again, and to keep refining.

Transformation is never linear. It builds in layers: from uncovering blind spots to stepping into confidence, from shaping culture to leading with legacy. Integration happens when those lessons stop living in separate chapters and start living together—awareness turning into practice, practice into influence, and influence into lasting impact.

Evelyn's story shows what that layering looks like across a career.

► EVELYN (Composite): The Arc of Integration

Evelyn, a composite drawn from several leaders I've coached, started her career in a small Midwestern store at 23, with a business degree and a sharp eye for process. Within a year, she was managing the store, and within three years, she was leading a district of ten.

She was precise. Relentless. Systems-driven. Execution-focused. And she got results.

By her mid-30s, Evelyn had become the "fixer" for a growing retail chain, sent to stabilize underperforming markets and standardize operations. When the company acquired a smaller competitor, she was tapped to lead the integration.

That's when her systems began to break down. Turnover spiked. Former employees from the acquired company left in droves. Her playbook wasn't landing.

"I gave them the answers," she said in our early coaching. "Why won't they execute?" she lamented.[6]

---

6 See also Chapter 2: "Blind Spots" and Chapter 4: "The Hidden Job Description," where we explored how technical mastery can mask unseen gaps in leadership influence.

Awareness

Evelyn's first realization came in a rural market. A store manager showed her how they had altered product displays to feature local farm goods. When Evelyn's integration team removed those items to standardize inventory, revenue dipped and community trust vanished.

"I realized I was imposing, not learning," she told me.

This was the turning point. Evelyn wasn't failing; she was outgrowing her old playbook. She began to listen, ask questions, and honor what she didn't yet understand.

Embodiment

She rewrote her approach. She built a hybrid strategy, one that protected brand consistency while honoring regional strengths. Metrics improved.

Years later, as SVP of Store Operations, she faced a new challenge: redefining convenience for a younger, digital-first customer. Her instincts told her to drive execution. But instead, she paused. She called her team together and asked a new kind of question:

"What do you see that I don't?"

That single question changed everything. She initiated flexible planograms, a digital ecosystem for ordering, and new employee development programs for Gen Z associates. She moved from tactician to strategist, and from fixer to facilitator.

Amplification

Evelyn eventually became CEO of the newly rebranded network, now operating more than a thousand stores.

She had grown the business, yes. But she'd also grown herself—and others. She launched internal mentorship circles. She spoke publicly but focused her stories on hard lessons more than wins. She became a visible advocate for sustainable retail practices. One of her proudest initiatives was a program offering entrepreneurial training to employees with aspirations beyond retail, celebrating their growth, even if it meant they left the company.

"Legacy isn't holding people," she said. "It's helping them launch."

Transmission

When Evelyn retired, her financials were impressive. But the numbers she cared about most looked like this:

- Thousands of employees had advanced from frontline roles to management.

- Hundreds had completed entrepreneurial training programs and had gone on to start their own ventures.

- Over a hundred communities had improved food access through her inventory reforms.

At her farewell celebration, a store manager who had once been a cashier stood up and said:

"She saw something in me when I didn't see it yet. And she showed me that leadership isn't about being perfect. It's about helping people rise, even if they're not sure they're ready."

That's integration in action. Not polish. Not perfection. But presence, reflection, and purpose lived across the span of a career.

The Integration Model: From Learning to Living It

Evelyn's story illustrates integration lived as steady recalibration across a career. She didn't abandon her strengths—she expanded them. That's what integration looks like over time.

Below are the four stages of integration I see most often in leaders I coach. Notice how each one builds on the other, not as a ladder to climb once but as layers you return to again and again. Take a moment to locate yourself: Are you building awareness, embodying new practices, amplifying others, or transmitting what you've learned?

STAGE	WHAT IT LOOKS LIKE	PRACTICES THAT REINFORCE IT
Awareness	Recognizing patterns, naming gaps	Feedback loops, coaching, honest reflection
Embodiment	Living the change consistently	Practice, repetition, behavioral shifts
Amplification	Influencing others through example	Mentoring, storytelling, cultural modeling
Transmission	Shaping systems and legacy	Succession planning, ecosystem building

Not every leadership arc is about system transformation. Some unfold in quieter, more personal ways, through resilience, consistency, and the steady refinement of presence. Here's what that looked like for one leader I've known for more than fifteen years.

► ERICA: From Self-Conscious to Sovereign Leader

Erica first walked into one of my professional presence workshops more than a decade ago. She was already deep into her career—a respected audit leader with eleven years of experience in finance and compliance. She had the credentials, the competence, and the work ethic. What she didn't yet have was confidence in how she came across.

After the session, she pulled me aside. "I know I'm good at my job," she said. "But I don't look the part. And I don't want that to hold me back."

She was raising two young children, navigating a divorce, and managing her career with discipline and steady drive. But she also knew that presence matters, and she wanted to lead with intention.

Over time, she began to transform how she showed up. She refined her communication. Invested in her physical presence. Lost weight. Reclaimed her health. But what stood out wasn't just how she looked; it was how she carried herself. She was becoming someone new—someone who aligned her external presence with her internal clarity.

From there, Erica moved into increasingly strategic roles: First at a global diagnostics company, then as Chief Audit Executive for a national retailer, and eventually into executive leadership at a major consumer brand, including a three-year assignment in Asia as a country leader.

Today, she's a senior executive in a male-dominated industry, one of the few women at the top of her organization. And after nearly thirty years in her profession, she leads with more conviction and clarity than ever.

But here's what I admire most: Erica has never led for herself alone. She invests in others. She notices emerging talent. She's sent multiple direct reports to me for coaching—not because they were struggling but because she believed in their potential.

That's integration.

She didn't just develop her image. She developed her presence. Then her leadership. And from there, her legacy.

Erica would be the first to say she's still growing. But these days, she's not asking, "Do I look like a leader?"

She's asking, "Who can I grow next?"

That's what integrated leadership looks like: built over time, fueled by vision, and sustained by care.

What Will Still Matter?

In a world increasingly shaped by AI, automation, and algorithmic decision-making, it's natural to wonder: What will leadership mean in the years ahead?

Here's the reality: Many operational tasks—even some once considered high-status—will be automated or augmented by artificial intelligence. But your presence will never be downloaded.

AI can summarize sentiment, but it can't feel when trust breaks or builds. It can generate a strategy deck in seconds, but it can't read the energy in a room or steady a team in uncertainty. It can predict behavior, but it cannot create belonging.

That's why integration matters more than ever. When technology accelerates, the leader's role is to slow down enough to connect the pieces—to ground yourself, embody steadiness, amplify others, and transmit trust.

Your most strategic asset won't be speed. It will be presence. Not perfection, but grounded clarity. And as the world accelerates, the leaders who remain steady will become the ones others rely on to make sense of it all.

 TOOL: The Monthly Leadership Mirror

Leadership alignment isn't a one-time achievement. It drifts. It needs attention. The best leaders I've coached don't assume they're set for life. They create regular checkpoints to stay true to how they want to show up.

This simple mirror can be used once a month. Take ten quiet minutes. Ask yourself these questions and write down your answers. Patterns will reveal where you've grown and where you're slipping back into old defaults.

1. **Am I leading from old patterns, or from awareness?**
→ Are your responses driven by habit or by thoughtful intention?

2. **What energy am I bringing into the room, and how does it land?**
→ Does your presence inspire calm, clarity, urgency, or confusion?

3. **Where is my voice most needed—and how am I using it?**
→ Are you leaning in when silence feels safer or stepping back when others should lead?

This isn't about judgment. It's about alignment. The mirror doesn't show perfection. It shows reality and gives you the chance to realign.

 ## COACHING CUE: Build Your Personal Board

Senior leadership can be lonely. The issue isn't unfriendly people—it's that rising through the ranks often shrinks your feedback loop. The most effective leaders I coach build what I call a **Personal Board of Directors:** a small, trusted group of truth-tellers who offer perspective, stretch your thinking, and remind you of your values when things get blurry.

Your board might include:

- A peer in another division who sees you clearly
- A mentor who knows your blind spots
- A former boss who still roots for your growth
- A direct report you trust for honesty
- A coach, advisor, or sponsor who challenges your comfort zone

Don't wait for a crisis to build your board. Curate it early—and keep it close.

READER-TO-LEADER

At the start of this book, you reflected on the version of yourself that fear was trying to protect. How has that version evolved?

Now ask yourself:

Reflect:

- Where am I most aligned in how I lead, and where do I still feel unfinished?

- How am I carrying the torch of presence today? Is it steady, unsteady, or hidden?

- Who around me is ready to carry the torch next?

Act:

- Choose one moment this month—one meeting, one decision, one conversation—to lead as an integrated leader: aware, embodied, amplifying, transmitting.

- Identify one person who could be part of your Personal Board of Directors. Reach out to them this week.

SPIRITUAL CUE: Return to Center

This chapter isn't just about succession. It's about transcendence—moving beyond self into something more expansive.

Ram Dass beautifully described the essence of meaningful leadership as *"walking each other home"*—a profound metaphor for guiding others while remaining on our own journey of growth. This path isn't about having all the answers or achieving perfection. It's a matter of presence, compassion, and the courage to stay open.

Whether it's Ram Dass reminding us to *"be here now,"* the Buddha teaching right action, or the Gospels inviting us to lead with compassion and courage, every tradition points to the same truth:

Great leadership starts within.

Every time you pause to listen, to center yourself, to connect deeply, and to choose with care, you are led from your deepest source. And in doing so, you become more fully yourself—and more fully a leader.

Leadership Truths: What Modern Leadership Requires

Before you go, here are the truths I hope stay with you. Not as techniques but as anchors and touchstones for how you show up.

- Leadership isn't a title. It's a presence.

- Presence matters more than polish.

- Confidence is not the absence of fear. It's the choice to show up anyway.

- Reflection is a leadership skill.

- Feedback is a gift. Self-awareness is a practice.

- Visibility is not vanity. It's a responsibility.

- Influence isn't loud. It's clear, consistent, and attuned.

- The tone you set travels faster than the words you say.

- Leadership is relational.

- If it's lonely at the top, you're doing it wrong.

- Legacy is built in moments, not milestones.

- The next level of leadership won't look like the last. Stay open. Stay human. Stay in the work.

REMEMBER THIS: *The work doesn't end.*

I want to say something directly to the leader you are now—and the one you're becoming:

The most common struggle I see in senior leaders isn't lack of skill. It's the illusion that development should be done by now.

You are never done.

You may need to carve out time for learning, welcome uncomfortable feedback, or step further into the "front of room" than feels natural. You may need to unlearn old instincts in order to meet the moment with presence.

That isn't failure. That's growth.

You are still being shaped. Keep choosing growth.

EPILOGUE
A Closing Thanks

Before we part, I want to thank you for the time and attention you've given to these pages.

My clients often ask, "What should I do to lead better?" The truth is leadership isn't only a set of skills. It's a way of being. That's what this book has tried to explore.

I often use a metaphor: imagine your leadership as a jigsaw puzzle. Each piece represents how others experience you—your energy, your expression, your decisions, your choices, even your silences. So many pieces. Some are large and easy to place. Others are subtle but essential. Every piece matters.

My work is to help you fit that puzzle together—authentically and intentionally.

I don't claim to have all the answers. But I've had the gift of working with incredible leaders, many across a decade or more, who return for coaching tune-ups when life changes, new roles emerge, or they want to sharpen their presence. The best leaders I know are the ones still asking questions.

I hope this book becomes a conversation between us—a place you can return to for reflection, reinforcement, or realignment. In the back of this book, you'll find tools, models, and references collected for you to revisit anytime you need them.

With deep appreciation for your leadership journey,
Kathryn Lowell

APPENDIX I
A Detailed Field Guide to Presence

This appendix is different from the rest of the book. The chapters you just read walked you through the coaching journey—how leaders shift from the inside out. What follows is the consultant in me speaking. It's a field guide: practical, tactical, and sometimes blunt.

You don't need to read it straight through. Treat it like a reference. Dip into the sections that matter most to you—visual presence, voice, difficult conversations, global etiquette. Pull out what you need when you're preparing for a high-stakes moment or when you want a quick reset on how others experience you.

I know this terrain well because I've lived it. I didn't grow up around fine dining or corporate rituals. My parents were loving and practical, but they didn't teach me which fork to use or how to navigate a boardroom dinner. My early finance career dropped me into those settings fast, and I had to decode the rules while keeping pace. Eventually, I became both an image consultant and an executive coach because I wanted to decode the unspoken rules—and show others how to use them without losing themselves.

This appendix is for professionals who may not have had access to those codes, whether because you didn't grow up around them, your culture has framed them differently, or your industry has not taught them. The point isn't to make you something you're not. It's to remove friction so your insight and leadership come through cleanly.

When polish is thoughtful and intentional, it becomes invisible. What remains is presence that's unmistakably yours—steady, credible and real.

VISUAL AUTHORITY
Framing Presence

Like it or not, people read you before they hear you. Your look either clears the path for your ideas—or makes them work twice as hard to land.

I can't tell you how many leaders I've had to speak with about what they've neglected (like eyebrows, nails, even nose hair!) These aren't cosmetic details—they're credibility cues. If they're distracting, people stop listening.

The silent cues that shape credibility include:

- Grooming (hair, nails, brows, beard, etc.)
- Fit (tailoring, hem length, sleeve length)
- Condition (scuffs, wrinkles, fading)
- Accessories (belts, bags, glasses, watch)
- Shoes (always read as a signal of care)

Your visual presentation either reinforces your leadership—or it undermines it. There is no neutral.

Your face is the star of the show: When people meet you, they don't remember your jacket first—they remember your face. Your clothes are the supporting cast, but your face holds the lead role. That's where trust is built, decisions are made, and leadership is felt. Everything you wear should frame and support your face. That means choosing colors and necklines that draw the eye upward. Avoid patterns or accessories that steal focus. Fashion as expression can work—if it's intentional. But if your outfit is louder than your insight, your ideas pay the price.

Fit is credibility: Tailoring is one of the simplest and smartest investments you can make. Off-the-rack can look custom with simple adjustments. The point isn't fashion—it's the signal your fit is sending. Clothes that sag, pull, or gape distract. Clothes that fit redirect focus back to your face and your message. A jacket that sits right on your shoulders says more about your leadership than the label inside.

Think cost-per-wear: Fast fashion is tempting—inexpensive and current—but it can look cheap quickly. Think about cost per wear, not sticker price. A $250 blazer worn weekly for five years costs far less per wear than a $49 blazer that pills or warps after two washes. Invest where your presence is most visible—on stage, on Zoom, in the boardroom. The pieces you rely on should feel like allies—ready when you need them, dependable in every setting. Credibility should never look disposable.

Garment care is leadership care. Even high-quality clothes look sloppy if neglected. Steam, brush, and check for lint. Wrinkles, odors, and pet hair may seem small, but they say you didn't plan. I'm a big fan of steaming garments—not just to remove wrinkles, but to refresh them between cleanings. It's faster and gentler than ironing, and it significantly extends the life of your clothing.

Silent Credibility Killers

- Clothes past their prime: frayed collars, pilled knits, stained or faded fabrics
- Visible underthings: bra straps, camis, undershirts—distracting, not edgy
- Sad shoes: scuffed toes, worn soles, rain damaged
- Slouchy bags or fraying belts: tired accessories drag your whole look down

- Overstuffed pockets. Bulging phones and keys distort your line and your polish.

These things whisper, "I didn't prepare." Which means your ideas must work twice as hard to be heard.

Visual Presence Isn't One-Size-Fits-All

Visual presence is always interpreted through a cultural lens. What looks "professional" in one setting may feel rigid or underdressed in another. Gender, ethnicity, religion, and geography all shape how visual cues are read.

A tailored blazer may signal confidence in New York and conformity in Nairobi. Bold lipstick might be celebrated in tech marketing and questioned in finance. Protective hairstyles, cultural garments, visible tattoos—these may express identity, not a lack of professionalism.

Visual polish should never erase who you are. It should align with the message you want to send. The goal isn't conformity. It's credibility, with integrity. Ask: "For whom? Where? And why?"

 TOOL: Garment Audit

Your wardrobe should feel like a strategic partner—not a graveyard of "maybe-someday" items. Let's get honest about what's still serving you. With a mirror, try on your go-to pieces and ask:

- Does this fit the leader I am today or a version I've outgrown?
- Does this frame my face—or fight for its attention?
- Do I look pulled together or pulled in three directions?
- Would I trust this version of me to carry a high-stakes meeting or represent me with senior leadership?

If the answer isn't a clear yes, it's a no in disguise.

Coaching Spotlight: When Casual Crosses the Line

Early in my image consulting career, business dress followed neat levels: casual, business casual, professional, formal. That framework worked then, but leadership style today is more complex. Expectations vary by industry, geography, generation, and role.

One thing hasn't changed: people still make snap judgments based on how you look. As dress codes have relaxed, there's real skill in doing casual well.

- Dark jeans? Great, if they fit and aren't sagging or shredding.
- Untucked shirt? Fine, it's cut to be worn that way—not over-sized or sloppy.
- Sneakers? Sometimes yes, but clean, sleek sneakers, not lawn-mowing shoes.

  Intentional casual says, "I'm approachable and polished." Unintentional casual says, "I rolled out of bed and hoped for the best."

READER-TO-LEADER

What one wardrobe upgrade would immediately align your presence with the leader you're becoming? Decide on it and make the change within the next week.

GROOMING
Small Details, Big Impact

Clothes set the frame, but grooming is what people notice up close. These details can support your message—or compete with it. Proper grooming is a form of self-respect and respect for others. It shows you value the role you're in and the people you're with.

In this section, we'll cover what gets noticed, what gets remembered, and how small tweaks can elevate your entire leadership presence.

Hair sets the tone. Long or short, natural or styled, textured or straight—what matters is that it looks cared for. A regular cadence (not the emergency cut when you can't stand it anymore) keeps attention on your ideas, not your overgrown edges.

One of the clearest shifts in professional image is facial hair. A well-kept beard now reads as modern and intentional. The difference is in the maintenance. What I often tell male clients is this:

Facial hair should look as manicured as the eighteenth green at Pebble Beach—not like you wandered in from a weekend camping trip.

If you've chosen to have a beard, you've chosen a routine. For those without facial hair, the same standards apply. A patchy shadow or uneven sideburns creates the impression that you didn't finish getting ready. Even slight neglect draws attention away from your message and onto your appearance.

And don't forget your brows. They frame your face more than anything else, especially on camera. Keep them neat and intentional—otherwise they become the headline.

If you color your hair, maintain it. Color is optional. If you choose to color, keep it consistent. Visible roots are more distracting than gray hair.

Skin matters more than you think. No one expects flawless, but cared-for skin reads as fresh and professional. A simple routine—cleanser, moisturizer, sunscreen—goes a long way. *Think of it as the executive version of stage makeup.* It's not about vanity; it's about visibility. Makeup is enhancement, not disguise. Done well, it helps your eyes register, your skin look even, and your expressions read clearly in the room or on camera. It doesn't have to be a production. I often teach clients a five-minute routine that's fast, effective, and professional. For men, even a dab of concealer or powder before going on camera is not unprofessional—it's practical.

The leadership smile. If facial hair norms have shifted, here's an even more pronounced change: the expectation of a confident, polished smile. At the executive level, it's assumed leaders will invest in dental care, whether it's orthodontia, whitening, or cosmetic work. Improving your smile isn't about vanity—it's about visibility. A well-cared-for smile doesn't just look good. It signals vitality, presence, and self-respect. I've worked with executives who avoided smiling in photos or held back in meetings because they were self-conscious about their teeth. Once they addressed it, their entire presence shifted—they became more open, more expressive, and more confident. It made them want to smile—and smiling is one of the most magnetic leadership signals you can send.

Hands are always on stage: As a leader, you gesture, pass documents, and shake hands. Ragged cuticles, chipped polish, or bitten nails pull focus fast. Neat, clean hands—polished or not—say you're well-kept and ready.

I once coached a finance director whose constant nail-biting (down to the nub) became the number one distraction colleagues mentioned in 360 feedback interviews. A couple of team members admitted they remembered his hands more than his points. Once he addressed the habit, the distraction disappeared, and the team was relieved.

Invisible signals: A subtle scent or fresh breath can leave a positive impression; too much can dominate the room. The rule of thumb: people should notice *you* before they notice your cologne, perfume, or gum.

Consistency Builds Credibility

Anyone can look polished once. But what earns respect is consistency. Set a personal standard for grooming and keep it there. People notice when you backslide—skipping trims, letting details slide, or showing up uneven. Inconsistency makes others wonder what else you're letting slip. Consistency signals steadiness they can count on.

Coaching Spotlight: What Personal Grooming Can Say

- Overgrown facial hair or chipped polish → "I may not manage detail well."

- Excessive makeup, scent, or styling → "I may lead with image over substance."

- Flaky scalp, food in teeth, or facial shine → "I'm not fully self-aware in key moments."

- Ungroomed brows, nose/ear hair → "I'm overdue for maintenance—and it shows."

- Clean, balanced grooming → "I take myself and this role seriously."

Grooming checklist. Do I consistently...

- Keep my hair clean, styled, and current?
- Groom facial hair (if applicable) or maintain a clean-shaven look that feels intentional?
- Care for my skin and nails regularly, not just reactively?
- Use makeup (if applicable) to enhance, not distract?
- Maintain fresh breath, clean teeth, and a subtle, pleasant scent?
- Understand how visible tattoos, piercings, or grooming choices may be perceived in my environment—and make my choices intentionally?

READER-TO-LEADER

Look in the mirror with curiosity. What's one grooming detail that no longer reflects the leader you're becoming? Commit to upgrading it this month with a schedule or professional help.

EMBODIED SIGNALS
Communicating Without Words

We've all heard the saying: "Actions speak louder than words." In leadership, it's more accurate to say: "Your body speaks first." Long before people hear your words, they're reading your posture, movement, expressions, and gestures.

Common Presence Leaks

We all have unconscious habits, especially when we're nervous or distracted, that chip away at our credibility. Here are the most common ones I see when I coach leaders:

- Slouching or collapsing posture → You may just be tired, but it reads as low confidence or disengagement.

- Fidgeting or restless hands → It leaks anxious energy and makes you look less in control.

- Looking at your phone during conversation → Even a quick glance comes across as disinterest or disrespect.

- Avoiding eye contact → Feels evasive or unprepared, no matter your intent.

- Flat or tense expression → Suggests stress or low warmth.

- Not smiling or nodding while listening → Often misread as disapproval.

- Turning your body away mid-conversation → Signals withdrawal.

- Standing too close or too far → Violates invisible boundaries and unsettles people.

Here's the hard truth: Intent doesn't matter. Interpretation does. The room is always reading you, and in a contest between your words and your body, the body wins.

The Executive Stance

When I'm working with clients on standing posture, whether it's a presentation, a panel, or just answering a tough question in a meeting, the hands are usually the giveaway. Nervous energy leaks fast, and I see it show up in three predictable ways:

- The fig leaf: Hands clasped in front, subconsciously guarding your parts. It's a common pose, but it reads as nervous and closed off, not exactly executive energy.

- The military clasp: Hands behind the back, surveying your troops. It looks stiff and dated, more parade ground than boardroom.

- The wandering T-Rex: Elbows pinned, gestures flickering awkwardly near the torso. Distracting at best, undermining at worst.

When I notice any of these, I'll often stop and say: "Drop your hands. Let them rest at your sides." At first it feels awkward—everyone tells me it does. But once they get used to it, gestures flow more naturally, and they appear more confident, open, and trustworthy. That's the move I coach for standing delivery: Hands at your sides, relaxed and ready. It's simple, but it changes everything.

What about when you're sitting? Here, hands should still be visible and intentional. Resting lightly on the table, holding a pen without fidgeting, or placed calmly in your lap works well. What doesn't work: crossed arms, hidden hands under the table, or constant fiddling with objects. The same principle applies—calm, open, intentional placement creates trust.

FIELD NOTE: Gesture Zones That Work

There's such a thing as "gesture geography." And like real estate, it's all about location:

- Too low (below the waist): You look like a penguin. Cute, but not convincing.

- Too high (above the chest): It starts to feel manic. Unless you're conducting an orchestra or casting a spell, lower your hands.

- The power zone (between navel and chest): This is where gestures land with authority. It's your communicative sweet spot.

Pro tip: Let your gestures support, not distract from, your message. Open palms signal transparency. A steady hand gesture can anchor a key idea. Less flapping, more meaning.

Space and Calibration: Reading the Room You're in

Another presence trap I often coach clients on is how they use space. In Western contexts, personal space hovers around eighteen to twenty-four inches. But that's not universal. It shifts with culture, context, and role. Too close? Feels intense. Too far? Feels like you're emotionally buffering.

And then there are the subtler missteps I call out in real time:

- Claiming the far edge of the table when you're supposed to be leading the meeting.

- Turning your body halfway out of a conversation, like you've already checked out.

- Hiding behind your laptop while others are connecting face-to-face.

- Facing your slides instead of your audience, as if PowerPoint needs reassurance.

These aren't just quirks. They're presence decisions, most made unconsciously. I once worked with a VP who consistently positioned himself at the corner of the conference table—never at the head, even when he was running the meeting. He thought it made him look collaborative. Instead, it confused the room about who was actually leading. Once he started claiming his seat at the table—literally—his team stopped looking around for direction. They looked to him.

I often see leaders miscalibrate their presence. With senior leaders, they lean back a little too far, trying to signal ease. Instead, it can look like lounging. Being too restrained with peers can read as cold. The fix? Calibrate for connection so your presence and message land as one.

TOOL: The Stand, Land, and Move Formula

When you're speaking while standing, whether it's a team update, an all-hands meeting, or a keynote, our delivery lives not just in your words, but in your movement. This simple sequence helps you anchor the room with clarity and control:

1. **Stand.** Begin in a grounded stance. Feet hip-width, shoulders relaxed, hands free.

2. **Land.** Deliver your core point while making solid eye contact. Hold one zone of the room if it's a larger group, or one person if it's a smaller setting.

3. **Move.** Shift your position purposefully after a key point, not mid-thought.

Owning the Room:
Movement, Message and Magnetic Delivery

By this point in the book, you surely understand that presence isn't just what you say; it's how you fill the space around you. Whether it's a boardroom, a ballroom, or a Zoom screen, the room reads you before you open your mouth.

When I'm coaching, I'll often stop a client mid-delivery and say: "Own the space you're in." That means move with purpose, not restlessness. When you stand to speak, plant your feet. When you walk, do it intentionally, not like you're trying to hit your step goal.

Want to really connect with the room? Pick a section of the audience (or one person in a smaller setting) and stay with them for a few beats. Here's the hard truth: Almost everyone rushes this part. Their eyes dart like a sprinkler, spraying attention across the room. It feels safer to keep moving, but it reads as scattered.

Holding still—really holding—will feel long to you, almost uncomfortable at first. But to your audience, it feels like focus, presence, and confidence. Those few extra beats give your words time to sink in. They let people absorb instead of chase.

If you rush the landing, you look anxious. If you hold it, you look commanding.

And please—unless you're doing stand-up comedy—no pacing. Pacing isn't presence. It's cardio. Plant, deliver, then move with intention.

Mirror Check: Are You Sending Mixed Signals?

Try this: Record yourself giving a sixty-second intro or delivering a point. Don't focus on the words; watch your body. Are you leaning too much? Shifting weight nervously? Repeating one odd gesture like a nervous tic?

Clients are often shocked when they see themselves for the first time. That "head nod thing"? That constant tug at your sleeve? The way you spin your ring every time you pause? Or the hair tuck, over and over like punctuation? It's all running on repeat. And it's fixable. Awareness is the first step to aligning your words and your body. Once you see it, you can't unsee it—and that's the point.

Physical alignment checklist. Do I consistently...

- Enter rooms upright and confident?
- Maintain eye contact when speaking and listening?
- Smile sincerely, not fixed or forced?
- Stay aware of how I take up space physically and interpersonally?
- Adjust my presence across cultures and power dynamics?

READER-TO-LEADER

What nonverbal habits might be undercutting your presence? Choose one behavior to observe and adjust over the next week.

Who do you know whose body language consistently radiates grounded presence—and what can you borrow from their good example?

VOCAL PRESENCE
The Sound of Leadership

Your voice is one of your most powerful leadership instruments—and one of the most neglected. Most people assume their voice is "just how it is." But it's a tool. Tone, pace, variation, and even silence shape how others receive your message, and whether or not they believe you.

What I often tell clients is this: monotone delivery drains energy from your message instantly. Your audience will disengage, no matter how good the content. On the flip side, racing breathlessly without pause feels overwhelming and amateurish. The goal is balance and modulation.

Try slowing down. Let your pitch rise and fall like punctuation—a comma, an exclamation point, a period. Use your voice the way you would underline a key idea, only where it matters.

Coaching Spotlight: Six Vocal Traps to Watch For

1. **The runaway train**: Talking so fast your message derails. Leaders who never pause sound rushed and reactive. Breathe. Pause. Land your point.

2. **The disappearing act**: Dropping your voice at the end of a sentence like you're apologizing for speaking. Authority trails off with it. Say it like you mean it, keeping your volume, projection and breath strong all the way through your thought.

3. **The up-talker**: Ending every sentence like it's a question? It makes solid ideas sound tentative.

4. **The one-note wonder**: Monotone delivery. Even great content sounds flat and forgettable when there's no modulation. Variation is what makes people stay with you.

5. **The vocal fryer**: That creaky, low-register rasp. It might feel casual or trendy, but it often reads as disengaged or insincere—especially across generations. (If you don't know what I'm talking about, search YouTube for any clip from *Keeping Up With the Kardashians*.)

6. **The over-explainer**: Rambling, repeating, or circling back until your clarity is buried. Just say it. Then stop talking. Leaders who over-explain sound like they're seeking permission, not offering direction.

Awareness is power. Most vocal habits are just patterns you've slipped into. And patterns can be updated. A little intention in your pacing, tone, and pauses can transform how people receive you.

Try this: Record yourself delivering a short intro. Don't judge the content; listen to the delivery. Are you rushing? Trailing off? Sounding uncertain? Once you notice, you can adjust.

TOOL: The Leadership Breath (What I Use Before I Speak)

I've done a lot of public speaking. And still, when I step up to deliver something that matters, my voice can shake. It's part nerves, part shallow breathing. If I'm not grounded, it shows.

Here's what most people try: one big breath in. But that quick inhale often creates tension—lifted shoulders, tight throat, shallow air.

Here's what I do instead, every time I speak:

- I exhale fully—pushing all the air out until there's nothing left.

- Not halfway. All the way. Push the air out. Push, push, push until there's nothing left.

- Then, without effort, my body draws in a deep, full breath. Automatically. My lungs fill completely.

And that's the breath I speak from. It gives volume without force. Resonance without tension. Most importantly, it carries me through my first couple of lines steady and strong, until I settle into my delivery.

When to use it:

- As you stand up to speak or step into a spotlight moment
- Right before delivering a key point
- Anytime your voice feels shaky, shallow, or rushed

This simple shift creates vocal steadiness and gravitas. I use it every time—not to sound polished, but to sound real. And believable.

Project—Don't Push

Strong vocal presence isn't about getting louder. True projection comes from breath. A well-supported voice carries without strain.

Speak from your diaphragm. Let the breath do the work. When you force sound from your throat, tension enters the room long before your message does.

When you're projecting correctly, your voice lands strong and steady—clear enough to reach the back row without ever tipping into a shout.

TOOL: The "Money Phrase" Technique

In every important message, whether giving feedback, pitching an idea or making a point, there's a **money phrase**: that part of the sentence that carries the real impact.

If you emphasize it intentionally, your message sticks. If you flatten it—or stress the wrong part—you risk being ignored, misunderstood, or tuned out.

Here's what I tell clients: Don't let the power leak out of your sentence. Find the phrase that matters most and land there.

Here's how the same sentence can land differently, depending on which phrase you emphasize and where you pause:

Example 1: Team recognition

"The way this team delivered under pressure was simply exceptional."

- If you stress "this team" → You'll emphasize collective pride
- If you stress "delivered under pressure" → You'll emphasize resilience
- Stressing "exceptional" → Emphasizes excellence

Coached version:
"The way **this team**...delivered under pressure...was simply **exceptional**."

Example 2: Delegation and trust

"You have full ownership of the final call, and I trust your judgment."

- Stressing "full ownership" → Highlights empowerment.
- Stressing "trust your judgment" → Builds confidence.

Coached version:
"You have **full ownership** of the final call—and I **trust your judgment**."

Example 3: Leadership accountability

"We need leaders who step up, not just show up."

- Stressing "step up" → Calls for active leadership.
- Stressing "not just show up" → Calls out passive behavior.

Coached version:
"We need leaders who **step up—not just show up**."

Practice tip: Before you speak, scan your notes and underline the money phrase.

Then, in delivery:

- Slow down slightly as you approach it.
- Drop your tone a half step to add weight.
- Pause briefly after you land it.

It's subtle, but powerful. And it's what makes people think, "You really meant that."

Vocal Energy = Leadership Energy

Monotone kills momentum. Overacting feels fake. What leaders need is **vocal flexibility**—the ability to adapt tone, volume, and pacing to match the moment.

A boardroom debrief isn't a rally. A panel discussion isn't a podcast. Know what the room calls for, and match your energy accordingly.

People have more sensitivity to your vocal energy than you may realize. In other words, if you sound rushed, they feel rushed. If you sound steady, they relax.

I once coached a director interviewing for a VP position. She was overqualified on paper, but her vocal energy came across as nervous—rapid-fire pace, rising inflection, tentative tone. We worked on slowing her delivery, dropping her pitch at the end of statements, and pausing before answering questions. The difference? She went from sounding like she was auditioning to sounding like she already had the role. She got the offer.

Verbal Presence—Less Filler, More Power

If you want to sound more intelligent, the fastest fix is simple: **stop cluttering your message with filler words.**

"Like." "You know." "I mean." "Actually." "Seriously." "So."

"Uh." "Um." "Hmm." All of these drain credibility and weaken clarity. At times fillers are used to buy time while your brain catches up, but just as often they are simply verbal tics.

When I review client presentations, I count the fillers. They're always stunned by the number. "It didn't feel like I said it that much." Exactly. It's unconscious.

Here's the good news. Just by bringing awareness to this pattern, people cut filler words by 70% to 80%. You don't need to eliminate them entirely, but you do need to trim them enough to let your message breathe.

Coaching Spotlight: The Verbal Tic Audit

Here's a quick exercise I give clients:

1. Record yourself presenting for two minutes.

2. Play it back. Each time you hear a filler, make a tally mark.

3. Look for repeat offenders. Everyone has a few.

4. Practice delivering the same message again—this time aiming to reduce the tally by half.

Bonus tip: When you feel a filler coming, pause instead. Silence is cleaner. You'll immediately sound more confident, more thoughtful, and in control.

Say It So They Get It

You may have great ideas—but if you mumble, slur, or swallow your words, your clarity disappears. In virtual meetings, it's even worse. Saying "quarterly projection" without crisp consonants becomes a blurry sound bite.

Precision matters. Good articulation requires intentional enunciating. My daughter is a vocalist, and her coach drilled into her: *"Diction is done at the tip of the tongue at the top of the* *teeth.*" It was both an exercise and a mantra. (Try saying that fast and you'll see why.)

Clear articulation demonstrates generosity to your listeners. It's a way of saying: I respect your time enough to be understood. If you want people to act on your words, let them hear every one.

The Pause: Use Silence as Strategy

We've already discussed how a pause beats a filler word every time. And in Chapter 9, we explored why the pause is one of a leader's strongest tools.

A well-timed pause deepens your authority. It communicates control, presence, and confidence—even under pressure.

What might seem like too long to you, feels *just right* to the audience. It gives them time to absorb your point and highlights what came just before.

Pause here:

- After a key idea → It lands harder.
- Before a rebuttal → It signals control.
- During a heated moment → It shows poise.

Silence isn't dead air. **It's power on mute.** If silence feels uncomfortable, remember this: the room is still listening. You don't have to rush to fill the air.

READER-TO-LEADER: Vocal Impact Checklist

Think of this as a mic check for leadership: if these aren't true, your voice isn't carrying the message.

Do I consistently...

- Speak clearly and at an appropriate volume?
- Vary pitch and pace to avoid monotony?

- Minimize filler words, such as I mean, um, like, and you know?
- Complete my thoughts without trailing off or ending on an upward inflection?
- Pause when needed, yield space, and land points with intention?

COACHING INSIGHT:

The more agile your voice, the more believable your leadership.

DIFFICULT CONVERSATIONS
Courage With Care

Some leaders confuse difficult conversations with confrontation. Others avoid them entirely and call it "being nice."

Here's the truth: your ability to navigate hard conversations—calmly, clearly, and without flinching—is one of the strongest indicators of leadership maturity.

 **COACHING CUE:** Avoidance wears a polite face, but it quietly erodes trust. If you don't face the difficult conversations, you aren't really leading.

Signs you're avoiding the real conversation

1. You rehash performance data , hoping the person *finally* gets it.
2. You leave meetings thinking, "Well, I kind of said what I meant..."
3. You drop hints instead of using direct language.
4. You vent to everyone, except the person who needs to hear it.
5. You delay the talk, then snap when your patience runs out.

Avoidance is just conflict on layaway. **You'll pay for it later, with interest.**

What Courage With Care Looks Like

Courage in tough moments isn't about who talks louder. And avoidance isn't care—it's sidestepping the truth.

A centered leader:

- Stays calm, not cold.
- Names what's real, not what's rehearsed.
- Uses brevity as strength.

Every hard conversation is a balance beam: truth on one side, relationship on the other. Courage with care means protecting both—not choosing one over the other.

And it's not just with your team. Some of the hardest conversations are upward:

- A peer who outranks you politically.
- A founder with blind spots.
- A senior leader whose behavior affects the team.

These moments test whether you can stay anchored when the hierarchy tilts against you. The challenge is the same: speak truth without losing trust.

Anchor phrases that help:

- "I want to raise something because I care about the impact on the team."
- "I respect your role here, and I'd like to share what I'm seeing on the ground."
- "This may be uncomfortable, but I think it's important to name."

Coaching Moves That Signal Maturity

Here are a few practices I use with clients navigating hard conversations:

- Set an intention: "My goal here is to be transparent and supportive—even if the message is hard to hear."
- Name the truth: "We've talked around this issue for a while, but I don't think we've said it directly."
- Hold steady: Let the silence do some of the talking. It gives the other person space—and shows you're not afraid of emotion.

- Stay with the person, not the problem: "I know this isn't easy to hear. I'm staying in this with you."

Coaching Story: The Almost Conversation

Leah, a senior director I coached, had a team member who consistently missed deadlines and deflected accountability. For six months, she danced around it. She gave indirect feedback. Reworded emails. Overcompensated for him in meetings.

When she finally addressed it directly, the team member was defensive and blindsided. "Why didn't you tell me sooner?"

Leah's insight was painful but powerful: "I thought I was being kind. But I was just being unclear—and unhelpful." From then on, she prepped hard conversations with two questions:

1. What's the truth I'm avoiding?

2. How can I say it without blame?

The shift was immediate. Her team described her as clearer, steadier, and more trustworthy.

Her takeaway was this: six months of hinting was more damaging than five minutes of honesty.

TOOL: Prepping for a Hard Conversation

Leah's breakthrough was simple: clarity doesn't happen by accident. It happens because you prepare for it.

Before the moment arrives, ground yourself in three steps:

1. **Breathe**. Drop your shoulders. Release any script.

2. **Clarify your intention**. Why does this matter? What outcome do you want?

3. **Visualize steadiness**. Imagine speaking with calm energy, not to win but to connect.

Even with prep, your body may react: a racing heart, tight throat, or mental blank. Notice it, but don't obey it. Let the discomfort move through without letting it run the show.

Extra tip: Say your opening line out loud once or twice. Hearing it in your own voice reduces nerves and helps you drop the script.

 ## COACHING INSIGHT: When You've Been Too Nice

Nice is safe. Nice is agreeable. But nice can also be evasive.

If people leave your conversations unclear, unmotivated, or confused about your expectations, you're not leading with kindness. You're leading with avoidance.

Clarity is kindness. Follow-through is respect. Together, they build trust.

Example: Saying "You're doing fine" when you know someone is struggling feels kind in the moment but leaves them unsupported. Saying, "I see where you're stuck, and I want to help you shift it" is clarity. Being kind this way helps.

 ## READER-TO-LEADER

What's one conversation you've been almost having but not quite?
- Write the one sentence you've been avoiding.
- Then ask: How could I say this with honesty, not caution?

CONVERSATIONAL RANGE
Leadership Beyond the Agenda

Many leaders are fluent in their domain, but when the conversation drifts beyond business, they falter. They smile politely, retreat to silence, or steer back to numbers. You can almost hear the conversational gears grinding down. Their intelligence may be high, but their range is narrow. And in leadership, narrow range limits influence.

Conversational range is the ability to speak thoughtfully across topics—art and ethics, global trends and generational quirks, culture and leadership. It's the ability to stay in the conversation, even when it's not your home turf.

Why It Matters

We want to do business with people we like and trust. And likeability and trust grow when you can meet others beyond the agenda.

- **Visibility:** In boardrooms, on panels, at dinner tables and press events, conversational range makes you more memorable and promotable.

- **Brand:** The best leaders are remembered not just for what they know, but for what they're curious about.

- **Opportunity:** Conversational agility creates openings—for mentoring, for influence, for recognition—because it signals readiness beyond your lane.

- **Relational capital:** People open doors for those who can connect across dimensions of life, not just business.

You don't need to be an expert. You just need to be conversant. Can you talk about Mark Rothko, the Federal Reserve, or a podcast you loved? Can you hold space in a conversation without hijacking it—or shrinking away? This kind of fluency signals leadership depth and positions you not only as an operator but as a visionary.

 TOOL: The Conversational Range Builder

Here are a few topic areas to keep in your back pocket:

- Art and culture → one artist, play, or creative trend
  Prompt: "Seen or read anything lately that surprised you?"

- Music → a favorite concert, genre, or new discovery
  Prompt: "What's been on your playlist lately?"

- Food and travel → a recent trip or go-to restaurant
  Prompt: "Anywhere you've eaten or traveled that I should know about?"

- Current events → one headline you've followed
  Prompt: "I've been wondering. What's your take?"

- Technology → a trend you're tracking (AI, Web3, etc.)
  Prompt: "Where do you see this trend impacting your world?"

- Literature → a book you've read or want to discuss
  Prompt: "Anything you've read recently that stuck with you?"

Conversational range can stretch from global policy shifts to sports, from wellness to sustainability—depending on the moment and the audience. Curiosity is enough. The more dimensions you can connect on, the more memorable—and promotable—you become.

It also prepares you for disruption. When the conversation shifts, whether it's AI, climate volatility, or a sudden cultural moment, leaders with range don't freeze. They engage. And that's often what sets them apart.

Generational Agility Is Conversational Range, Too

Conversational range also means knowing how to speak across age, culture, and context.

At sixty-one, can you mention TikTok or *Love Island* without rolling your eyes and still sound like yourself?

At twenty-one, can you talk about interest rates, inflation, or workplace history with a boomer client—and listen without overcompensating?

Generational agility is simply range applied across time. Leaders who practice it build bridges instead of gaps. A shared laugh, a well-placed question, or a brief learning moment can turn hierarchy into rapport and colleagues into collaborators. These everyday bridges are what workplace culture is actually made of.

Sushi, Chopsticks, and Cultural Curiosity

The first time I ate sushi, I was on a business trip. This was before sushi went mainstream—back when it still felt daring to most Americans. I didn't know how to use chopsticks, and I'd never eaten raw fish. Thankfully, the host ordered for the table. I watched. I mimicked. I composed my face. And I got through it.

Now? Sushi is my favorite food. I seek out food tours when I travel. That moment of discomfort gave me access to something bigger—new tastes, new confidence, new conversations.

That's what conversational range offers, too. You don't need to lead every conversation. You just have to stay in it. Range doesn't come from knowing everything. It comes from being curious enough to stay present, learn, and connect.

READER-TO-LEADER

Reflection

- What's one area—outside your expertise—where you feel underconfident, and when was the last time you stayed silent because of it?

Action

- This week, get curious in that area: read something new, ask a question, or listen to someone else's perspective.
- In your next conversation, practice staying present instead of retreating or deflecting.

RELATIONAL PRESENCE
(Especially for Introverts)

In the previous section, we explored conversational range—the ability to speak across a variety of big-picture topics. But leadership presence isn't only about breadth of knowledge. It's about **relational depth**.

How you show up in unscripted, informal moments speaks volumes, especially if you're not the type who leads with volume. Presence shows most in how you connect, not how much you say.

Small moments—elevator rides, post-meeting conversations, hallway chats—can deepen trust or drain it. For many introverts, these in-between moments are the hardest to navigate. There's no clear script, no defined goal, and often no time to recharge before or after. The pressure to be "on" can make even small talk feel like a performance, when all you really want is an honest exchange.

The good news? You don't have to fake connection to build it. Small, genuine gestures go a long way in helping people feel seen—and that's true for everyone, not just introverts.

Personal Note: I'm an Introvert, Too

Here's my reveal: I'm an introvert who masquerades as an extrovert. I can work the room, public speak, and stay fully present with my clients—but by the end of the day, I'm ready to collapse on the couch. Fully depleted. Don't even talk to me.

I've coached plenty of thoughtful, accomplished introverts who feel the same way. They don't want vague advice like "just be yourself." They want specifics—clear conversational cues they can prepare, practice, and rely on.

This isn't about becoming someone else. It's about having the tools to show up as yourself—without feeling like you're performing.

So what does that look like in practice?

Conversation Cues That Build Trust

- Start with warmth and curiosity.

- Ask open-ended questions that invite others in.

- Balance speaking and listening instead of dominating or disappearing.

- Exit conversations with grace, not apology.

- Navigate small talk in a way that still feels like you.

- Avoid softening every statement ("just," "kind of"); take a clear stand.

- Make space for quieter voices to be included.

Exiting With Ease

Most people—introverts especially—struggle with exits. We either bolt abruptly or overexplain.

I'll admit, I've been known to vanish from parties when my social battery hits zero. Sometimes that's the introvert's version of crowd management. But in professional settings, graceful exits matter. They close loops and leave good energy behind.

You can do that with small cues that communicate respect and completion:

- "I'm going to let you circulate—thanks so much for the conversation."

- "I need to catch someone before they head out, but this was great."

- "I'm going to refresh my drink and say hi to a few people. I really enjoyed talking with you."

- "I don't want to monopolize your time, but I'm glad we connected."

If the setting allows, use body language too. Step back slightly, smile, and make soft eye contact before you turn.
The key: be warm, be brief, and don't apologize.

Leaving well is an energy skill. Exits aren't about escaping; they're about ending with presence. When you depart smoothly, you preserve connection—and your own capacity to reengage later.

Conversation Starters That Work

If you dread small talk, you're not alone. Here are a few starters that feel natural, open, and useful, without being intrusive or cliché:

- "What's been the highlight of your week?"

- "What's something you're working on that excites you?"

- "Is there a book, podcast, or idea you've been chewing on lately?"

- "What helps you reset after a high-pressure stretch?"

- "What's one thing you've learned recently that surprised you?"

I worked with a VP who felt paralyzed at networking events— she never knew what to say. I gave her one question to carry in her back pocket: 'What's been taking up your energy lately?' It's open-ended, genuinely curious, and gets people talking. Six months later, she said, 'I don't dread these anymore. I just ask the question and listen.'

For Introverts: Connection Without the Spotlight

You don't have to be witty. You just have to be warm.

Here are some practical strategies that work:

- Set a goal: one meaningful exchange over three superficial ones.

- Prep a few openers and closers (e.g., "So glad we got to connect").

- Focus on curiosity rather than trying to be charismatic.

People remember how you made them feel, not how clever you were.

After social interactions, give yourself time to recalibrate. This isn't withdrawal; it's refueling. **Build social stamina gradually.** The temptation to skip networking events, group dinners, or drop-ins is real. But presence isn't built from avoidance—it's built from gentle exposure. Don't force yourself to stay all night. Just go for 30 minutes. *Thirty minutes.* Show up, make one sincere connection, then leave with your energy intact.

In large gatherings, focus on depth over reach. One genuine conversation will sustain you more than ten surface greetings. Energy management is presence management.

One of my clients—a self-acknowledged introvert—realized she was better at depth than breadth. Instead of working the room at large events, she started scheduling 20-minute coffee chats after key meetings. Smaller, quieter, more meaningful. Her peers started describing her as 'incredibly connected'—not because she was everywhere but because when she showed up, she was fully present.

I can attest to this: over time, you will find your tolerance grows. You might even eventually enjoy it.

BUSINESS DINING
It's Not About the Food

Let's be clear: a business meal is a meeting. It just happens to come with menus and silverware. You're not there for the great steak. You're there to connect, communicate, and build trust.

What I often tell clients is this: you're not at lunch. You're at work—with utensils. Done well, a meal can accelerate rapport more than three scheduled Zooms ever could. Done poorly, it can quietly raise doubts about your judgment, presence, or social fluency.

How to Show Up at the Table

Whether it's a casual lunch with a peer, a client dinner at a white-tablecloth restaurant, or a global event with formal cultural norms, your presence still communicates. What changes is the context—the tone and tempo, not the leadership signals.

Presence questions to consider:

- Am I gracious and prepared, or rushed and reactive?
- Do I engage everyone, or just the most senior person at the table?
- Do I read the moment, or dominate it?
- Do I leave others feeling elevated, or overlooked?

Before the meal:

- Look up the restaurant in advance; know the dress code and tone.
- Prep etiquette if you're unsure. Quiet confidence comes from preparation.
- Ground yourself: a few slow breaths before walking in resets your energy.

During the meal:

- Follow the host's lead when ordering or beginning to eat.

- Avoid the priciest or messiest dish.

- Match the most restrained person at the table—or go lower.

- Keep your phone out of sight; eye contact matters more than ever.

- Invite quieter voices into the conversation.

- Be ready to talk beyond work—but don't over rehearse it.

After the meal:

- Thank the host (or the most senior person) with sincerity.

- If you build rapport, follow up with a short thank-you message.

- If you hosted, pay discreetly—don't make it a production.

Every meal serves the same purpose. Is this a relationship-building moment, a business milestone, or a soft negotiation? The better you read the tone, the more aligned your presence becomes.

Navigating Drink and Toasts

This comes up often with clients. You're at a dinner. Wine is being poured. A toast is coming. What now?

You don't owe anyone an explanation. "Just water for me" is enough. Raise your glass—even if it's sparkling water—when others toast. If someone orders for the table, it's fine to quietly request non-alcoholic pairings. You don't have to make it a moment. Just move on gracefully.

When it comes to wine moments, you don't need to be a sommelier, but you do need to navigate smoothly.

- If you drink, know your limit before you walk in. Sip slowly. Don't refill unless the host does.

- If you don't drink, hold the glass for the toast, smile, touch the glass to your lips, and move on.
- If asked for your opinion, a graceful deferral works: "That sounds great—you know far more than I do."

Confidence isn't ordering the best bottle. It's knowing how to stay comfortable at the table.

Hosting With Presence

When you're the host, the etiquette shifts. You set the tone—formally or informally. A great host makes the room feel easy, even when the setting is formal.

As host, you are responsible for:

- Choosing a venue that fits your guest's comfort and culture.
- Communicating dress expectations if needed.
- Review the menu first to set the pace, but let your guests order before you.
- Letting your guest begin the conversation.
- Ensuring everyone is included, served, and heard.

Phrases that make meals easier:

"I'd love your recommendation." (for wine)

"Jordan, I'd love your take on this." (to include a quiet voice)

"I want to be mindful of your time—shall we wrap up?" (to close gracefully)

"Excuse me just a moment—please keep going, I'll be right back." (to step away discreetly)

Avoiding the Pitfalls

Even seasoned professionals make etiquette missteps. Here are a few to stay ahead of:

- Ordering before others → rushed.

- Overexplaining preferences → self-focused.

- Jumping into business too soon → relational miss.

- Fumbling payment → unclear on norms.

- Treating the meal as pitch time → transactional, not relational.

These slips won't ruin a meal, but they do shape how others read your professionalism and poise.

What They'll Remember

In the end, what people remember isn't the food. It's how you made them feel. These are the cues that quietly shape your reputation.

SIGNAL	WHAT IT SAYS
Arriving early and composed	"I take this seriously."
Letting others speak freely	"I don't need to dominate to be credible."
Managing alcohol intake	"I regulate well under pressure."
Not checking your phone	"I know how to be fully present."
Bringing others into conversation	"I notice who's not being heard."
Warm thanks to the host	"I see people, not just power."
Following up with a personal touch	"I build real relationships, not just rapport."

That's the goal: confident, gracious, attuned—the kind of presence that builds trust at any table.

EVERYTHING SPEAKS
The Overlooked Signals

Not every part of your leadership presence walks in with you. Much of it happens offstage—through your space, your timing, your responsiveness, and the habits you show when no one's watching.

Professional polish isn't just about what you wear. It's how you show up across every dimension of interaction—especially in those moments you think don't matter. These cues are subtle, often overlooked, and absolutely consequential. Because when leaders rise, **everything speaks.**

Your Space Speaks

Your physical environment signals how you work, focused or scattered, intentional or improvised. In a hybrid workplace, people literally see into your space.

Ask yourself:

- What's visible behind me on camera—calm or clutter?
- Do lighting, background, posture, and camera framing elevate me, or distract?
- Do I bring the same intention to my workspace as I do to my appearance?

Quiet detractors: chaotic background, harsh lighting, distracting objects, domestic clutter in frame, unmanaged noise, or backdrops that pull focus away from you.

A clean, intentional space says: I'm present. I'm prepared. I'm here to engage.

Five-Minute Space Reset

1. Clear the frame → one neutral backdrop or tidy shelf

2. Light your face → lamp at eye level, avoid overhead shadows

3. Raise the lens → camera at eye height, arm's-length away

4. Sound check → mute notifications; avoid jangly jewelry or noisy objects

5. Posture check →feet grounded, shoulders easy, face framed

The Physical Language of Trust

Sound travels. Noisy jewelry, jangly keychains, or squeaky shoes can undermine an otherwise polished presence. How you handle objects matters, too—fiddling with pens, flipping papers, or checking your phone sends signals about your internal state, often without you realizing it.

Warmth is felt. A clammy handshake, a limp grip, or an uncomfortable interaction is often remembered more vividly than your title.

The Handshake Still Speaks

The handshake remains one of the last physical rituals of business—and one of the fastest trust cues we have left in professional culture. In a digital-first world, it stands out as physical, personal, and full-spectrum. It engages almost every sense:

- Touch: Firm, not aggressive. Warm, not clammy. Steady, not rushed.

- Sight: Direct eye contact, focused presence. No darting eyes and drifting attention.

- Sound: Your vocal greeting sets the energy as clear, confident, and friendly.

- Scent: Close range means hygiene (and subtle fragrance) will be noticed.

Common mistakes:

- The limp fish—reads as discomfort or lack of self-trust.
- The bone crusher—overcompensates with dominance.
- The two-hand trap—can feel overly intimate or performative.
- The lingering grasp—shifts the energy from mutual to manipulative.

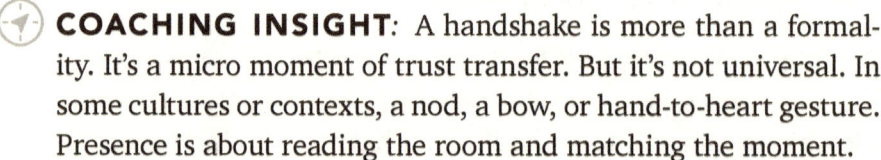 **COACHING INSIGHT:** A handshake is more than a formality. It's a micro moment of trust transfer. But it's not universal. In some cultures or contexts, a nod, a bow, or hand-to-heart gesture. Presence is about reading the room and matching the moment.

Digital Signals: Your Public Footprint

In today's connected world, your online presence often introduces you. A quick Google search, a LinkedIn profile, or even an outdated company bio can shape perception instantly. Silent impressions are forming whether you intend them or not.

Ask yourself:

- Is my headshot current, professional, and well-composed?
- Does my LinkedIn reflect who I'm becoming, not just what I've done?
- Have I reviewed my digital trail (search results, old content, outdated bios)?
- Could anything I reshared or posted undercut how I want to be perceived?
- Am I visible in the right spaces for my industry or sphere of influence?

Your digital footprint is a leadership asset. Manage it as carefully as you manage your in-room presence. Everyone has a data trail, so make a habit of searching yourself regularly. If outdated or irrelevant content surfaces, there are services and processes to help remove or update it. Every search result and profile is a trust cue. Make sure it's one you intend to send.

Quiet Behaviors That Signal Maturity

Some of the most trusted leaders aren't the loudest. They earn credibility through small consistent signals.

- Showing up on time and prepared → "I respect your time and mine."

- Keeping meetings focused and inclusive → "I make meetings count."

- Avoiding gossip or sarcasm → "I can be trusted in the room— and beyond."

- Staying off your phone during one-on-ones → "I know how to be present."

- Sharing thoughtful content online → "I think before I post."

- Thanking the room or support staff → "I value others—even when no one's watching."

Polish is revealed in how you treat your tools, your space, and your people. Leaders who earn quiet trust are the ones who show care in the smallest details.

Presence also shows up in how you relate. Not in the big speeches, but in the unscripted, everyday interactions that deepen confidence or quietly weaken it. For many leaders, especially introverts, this can feel like the hardest part of presence to master.

The Amplifier Effect: Visibility Beyond the Spotlight

As leaders rise, even casual words and small behaviors carry farther than intended. What once felt like a throwaway line or a quick email now carries disproportionate weight. The same sentence that felt harmless two levels ago can shake confidence when it comes from a VP.

That's the amplifier effect: your words and actions echo farther than you think. You don't need to weigh every word—only recognize that they now weigh more.

Leadership maturity isn't just tested in keynotes and boardrooms. It's revealed in the daily. How you run a meeting, respond to pressure, or acknowledge the people around you. Professionalism lives in the in-between moments.

Everyday Presence Checklist

A quick self-audit for the quiet cues that shape perception.

- Start and end meetings on time?

- Acknowledge people's work formally and informally?

- Hold space with discretion or drift into gossip and venting?

- Stay off my phone during real conversations?

- Post, email, or forward content with clear intent?

- Treat staff, servers or interns with visible respect, even when rushed?

- Move through space with intention, knowing my body is always narrating my leadership.

READER-TO-LEADER: The Everything Speaks Audit

Your presence isn't just how you show up when you're "on." It's how you're experienced in the margins—through space, rhythm, behavior, and tone.

Choose one signal to refine this week. Because even the quietest cues are saying something.

GLOBAL PRESENCE
Respect That Travels

Executive presence doesn't stop at borders. It travels with you.

And how it lands depends less on knowing every rule and more on showing up with humility, respect, and cultural attunement. Global sophistication is the willingness to adjust and to learn.

In today's connected world, many leaders find themselves working across cultures: hosting international clients, leading global teams, or representing their organization abroad. The rules may change, but your presence still matters. And when presence crosses borders, curiousity becomes your greatest asset.

A Story from Oman

Years ago, I was invited to deliver image training for the Oman Oil Company. The team was gracious, elegant, and impeccably attired in traditional dishdasha and abaya. Their warmth was immediate, and their hospitality unforgettable.

That evening, my colleague and I (both women) were invited to the home of a senior executive. We were escorted into a private women's reception area, where a lavish buffet awaited us: platters of lamb, rice, dates, flatbreads, and sweets—more food than two people could possibly eat. Every dish had been prepared with care and intention.

We didn't meet her husband or any male family members, something I later learned was a reflection of respect, not exclusion. Her invitation, the meal, and the privacy were a gift.

I didn't speak Arabic. I didn't know the customs. But I listened. I asked. I expressed gratitude. And that mattered as much as perfect etiquette ever could.

That night reminded me of something I've carried into every

global situation since: people remember less whether you get every detail right, and more whether you show gratitude, presence, and genuine respect.

Later that evening, we were presented with Omani-made gifts: a set of elegant napkin rings and a bottle of perfume—generous, thoughtful, and deeply cultural. It reminded me that sometimes the most sophisticated response is to simply receive hospitality with gratitude, without needing to match it. Just honor it.

Presence Doesn't Always Translate

Before you assume your leadership style carries globally, pause. Cultural cues vary dramatically. A show of confidence in one region may register as arrogance in another. Efficiency in one meeting might feel rushed and disrespectful elsewhere.

What feels normal to you may signal something very different elsewhere. Casual dress can be seen as disrespectful or sloppy. Direct feedback may land as public shaming. Rapid small talk may feel superficial. First-name use can come across as disregarding hierarchy. Fast decision-making might be interpreted as arrogance or unnecessary risk-taking.

The point is simple. Professionalism doesn't look the same everywhere. Before you assume your default is universal, pause. Ask yourself: What assumptions do I carry about "professionalism" that might not be shared in this room?

Global Awareness Is Executive Presence

The leaders who earn global respect aren't the ones who know every rule—they're the ones who stay curious. Presence travels best when it signals humility, adaptability, and respect.

Ask yourself: Do I research cultural norms before major meetings or travel? Do I adapt without fuss? Do I treat differences as a threat—or as a chance to learn?

Signals and Questions That Travel Well

A few behaviors signal respect almost anywhere:

- Wait before eating or toasting → "I understand this is ceremonial."
- Dressing in alignment with the context → "I'm aware I'm not the center."
- Use your right hand for greetings or gifts where it matters → "I've done my homework."
- Asking curious, respectful questions → "I want to understand—not impose."

And when you're unsure, don't fake it. Ask respectfully. Simple questions earn trust:

- "Would you prefer I remove my shoes?"
- "Are there gestures I should be aware of?"
- "Is there anything I should understand about how this meeting will begin?"

You don't need a script. You need the courage to ask. That's what earns you trust in rooms you don't fully understand yet. The same principle applies to gifts and hospitality.

In some cultures, gifts are expected. In others, they're discouraged or even prohibited. The same goes for receiving generous hospitality. When in doubt:

- Check company policies (yours and theirs).
- Don't over-reciprocate; grace matters more than value.
- Ask a trusted local colleague if you're unsure.
- If you must decline a gift or a certain food, do it gently and with gratitude.

That same evening in Oman, after the unforgettable dinner, we were presented with Omani-made gifts: a set of elegant napkin rings and a bottle of perfume. The gifts weren't flashy. They were generous, thoughtful, and deeply cultural. And they reminded me that sometimes the most sophisticated response is to simply receive hospitality with gratitude, without needing to match it. Just honor it.

Global polish isn't rigid. It's relational.

Communication Across Cultures

Language carries more than words. What feels clear or confident in one culture may come across as blunt, rushed, or even dismissive in another. A few reminders:

- "Yes" doesn't always mean yes—it may mean "I hear you" or "I don't want to disagree."
- Volume, speed, and tone translate differently across regions.
- In some cultures, silence signals thoughtfulness—not discomfort.
- When working with interpreters, speak clearly, pause often, and make eye contact with the person—not the interpreter.

Even seasoned leaders misread the room globally. Some common missteps include:

- Assuming silence means agreement.
- Prioritizing speed over trust.
- Missing the value of relationship-building time.
- Framing feedback or conflict too bluntly.
- Assuming your style of urgency is shared.

Global presence requires slowing down, listening longer, and noticing more. Sophistication is knowing when to pause—even if you're right.

READER-TO-LEADER

Which global dynamic do you need to sharpen? This week, try one of the following:

- Ask a colleague from another culture what they wish more global leaders understood.
- Research a holiday, value, or communication norm different from your own.
- Watch a 10-minute video on etiquette in a country where you do business.

Global presence isn't flawless execution. It's the small signals that say: I see you, I value you, and I'm willing to learn.

Case Studies in Executive Polish Transformation

These stories illustrate what happens when polish evolves into presence. They are composites drawn from real coaching engagement, showing how small refinements in image, behavior, and energy can unlock powerful shifts in leadership.

► DEV: The Polished Introvert

Dev, a technical VP, was highly accomplished but quiet and often faded into the background in cross-functional meetings. His grooming and presence were neat but understated. Through coaching, we worked on his posture, voice, and connection skills.

Rather than trying to be loud, he practiced being steady. He set a goal to contribute one bold insight per meeting and, instead of retreating, he followed it with a short, well-placed question that invited others in. Over time, he also prepared one story or example to illustrate a key point without overtalking it.

His peers started turning to him for strategic input—not just technical answers.

► ANGELA: Reclaiming Executive Credibility

Angela, a high-performing senior leader, hit a wall after relocating globally. Her new team found her too casual and abrupt.

Through coaching, we re evaluated how tone, pacing, and attire played in her new region. She began adopting local norms, such as more formal greetings, a polished appearance, and slower, more deliberate speech. She didn't abandon her authentic self; she expanded it. Within months, her credibility returned. She was invited to join the regional advisory board. More importantly, her team began to trust not just her capability, but her cultural awareness and respect.

► **ETHAN: From Draining to Sustainable Presence**

Ethan, a senior product leader, was brilliant but exhausting. His intensity filled every room—fast-paced, restless, relentless. At first, colleagues admired his drive, but over time they described him as "draining." Meetings ended with people tired instead of motivated.

Through coaching, Ethan began to recalibrate. He built recovery into his schedule, shortened his contributions, and learned to ground himself before entering a room. Instead of showing up depleted and wired, he showed up steady and intentional.

The result? His presence shifted from overwhelming to sustainable. Colleagues stopped avoiding him and started seeking him out. Ethan discovered that energy, like polish, speaks and that presence is most powerful when it's steady.

The Common Thread: Dev found his voice. Angela expanded her cultural credibility. Ethan regulated his energy. Their paths were different, but the lesson was the same: polish evolves into presence.

Presence isn't about adding more. It's about refining what's already there, until people stop noticing the surface and start trusting the substance. That's when leadership takes hold.

CONCLUSION
From Polish to Presence

The appendix to this book was never just about wardrobe, grooming tips, or etiquette rules. It's about alignment between who you are and how others experience you.

Executive polish is the outward expression of inner clarity. It's the signal that says: "I take this seriously. I know who I am. I'm here to connect." When your presence is intentional, your message lands with power, your leadership feels steady, and others trust what they see.

Think of polish as the infrastructure—not the performance. It's the structure that frees your energy to focus on what matters: credibility, care, and contribution. When polish becomes second nature, it stops being a checklist. You stop obsessing over the surface and start connecting with substance.

And that's when the shift happens. You stop managing how you're seen. You get over yourself and into Second Circle—grounded, connected, and fully present with others.

You become relational. Awake. Resonant.

That's the presence people trust.

That's the moment polish becomes invisible—and leadership begins.

A Final Word: Presence as Freedom

Presence isn't about looking expensive. It's about leading with care. Quiet power. Attention to detail. Respect for self and others.

And here's the secret: the more refined your polish, the more freedom your presence holds.

You stop managing perception and you start making impact.

When you show up clear, intentional and grounded—you don't just look like a leader.

You are one.

APPENDIX II

Quick Reference for Everyday Presence

I offer the following as quick references—tools I return to often in coaching. Think of them as touchstones you can scan when you need a reset.

The Power of First Impressions

People form lasting impressions in under a second. Once formed, those impressions color how everything you do is interpreted—your competence and warmth, and readiness for the next level.

Visual cues

- Dress for the level you want—not just the one you're in.
- Keep grooming and clothing clean, current, and purposeful.
- Posture signals openness and confidence, not collapse or overcompensation.
- Facial expression matches the tone of the room: grounded, warm, and attuned.

Vocal cues

- You speak with a grounded tone, not rushed, breathy, or flat.
- Let your vocal energy support the message, not overpower it.
- Pause and let key points land.

Energetic presence

- Enter with calm clarity.
- Take up space without fidgeting or shrinking.
- Let your energy say, "I'm here with purpose."

Digital signals

- Your Zoom setup is clean, well-lit, and distraction-free.
- Your email and messaging tone is professional, clear, and confident.
- Your digital footprint reflects the leader you are becoming.

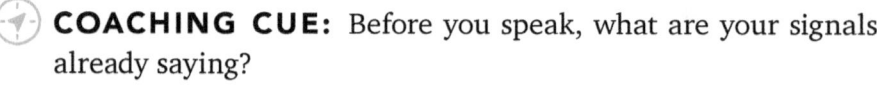 **COACHING CUE:** Before you speak, what are your signals already saying?

7 Signals of Leadership Energy

You're always transmitting. The question is: Are you doing it on purpose?

ENERGY DIMENSION	HOW IT SHOWS UP	WHY IT MATTERS
Physical Presence	Posture, stillness, movement, breathing rhythm	Signals steadiness (or tension) before you speak
Emotional Tone	Facial expression, vocal tone, micro-reactions, emotional availability	Creates safety or caution in others
Mental Clarity	Pacing, focus, organization, coherence	Shapes trust in your thinking and discernment
Intentionality	Presence vs. distraction, verbal congruence	Reveals whether you're leading the moment or lost in it
Containment	Ability to hold discomfort without leaking it	Builds calm authority under pressure
Relational Energy	Attunement, empathy, responsiveness	Influences team trust, openness, and motivation
Cultural Frequency	The tone you reinforce (urgency, blame, steadiness)	Quietly builds or erodes the team climate

REFERENCES

Chapter 1: Fear in the Climb

– Bravata, Dena M., Sharon A. Watts, Autumn L. Keefer, et al. "Prevalence, Predictors, and Treatment of Impostor Syndrome: A Systematic Review." *Journal of General Internal Medicine* 35(4): 1252–1275, 2020.

– LeDoux, Joseph. *The Emotional Brain: The Mysterious Underpinnings of Emotional Life.* Simon & Schuster, 1996.

Chapter 2: Blind Spots

– Eurich, Tasha. "What Self-Awareness Really Is (and How to Cultivate It)." *Harvard Business Review,* 2018.

– Luft, Joseph and Harrington Ingham. "The Johari Window: A Graphic Model of Interpersonal Awareness." Proceedings of the Western Training Laboratory in Group Development, UCLA, 1955.

– Rilke, Rainer Marie. *Letters to a Young Poet.* Translated by M. D. Herter Norton. W.W. Norton & Company, 1934.

Chapter 3: The Confidence Illusion

– Cuddy, Amy. *Presence: Bringing Your Boldest Self to Your Biggest Challenges*. Little, Brown Spark, 2015.

– Dass, Ram. *Be Here Now*. Lama Foundation, 1971.

– Dunning, David and Justin Kruger. "Unskilled and Unaware of It: How Difficulties in Recognizing One's Own Incompetence Lead to Inflated Self-Assessments." *Journal of Personality and Social Psychology*, 77(6): 1121–1134, 1999.

– Rodenburg, Patsy. *Presence: How to Use Positive Energy for Success in Every Situation*. Penguin Books, 2008.

Chapter 4: The Unspoken Rules of Rising

– Cuddy, Amy. *Presence: Bringing Your Boldest Self to Your Biggest Challenges*. Little, Brown Spark, 2015.

– Willis, Janine and Alexander Todorov. "First Impressions: Making Up Your Mind After a 100-Ms Exposure to a Face." *Psychological Science*, 17(7): 592–598, 2006.

Chapter 5: Leading Across

– Cullen, Kristin L., Charles J. Palus, and Craig Appaneal. *Developing Network Perspective: Understanding the Basics of Social Networks and Their Role in Leadership*. Center for Creative Leadership (White Paper), 2013.

– Edmondson, Amy C. *The Fearless Organization: Creating Psychological Safety in the Workplace for Learning, Innovation, and Growth*. Wiley, 2018.

Chapter 6: The Energy Shift

– Dass, Ram. *Be Here Now*. Lama Foundation, 1971.

– Lao Tzu. *Tao Te Ching: A New English Version*. Translated by Stephen Mitchell. Harper & Row, 1988.

– LinkedIn News. "Generational Workplace Trends: Mental Health and Boundaries." *LinkedIn News*, 2023.

– Schwartz, Tony and Catherine McCarthy. "Manage Your Energy, Not Your Time." *Harvard Business Review*, 2007.

Chapter 7: When the Work Changes

– Lao Tzu, *Tao Te Ching: A New English Version*. Translated by Stephen Mitchell. Harper & Row, 1988.

Chapter 8: Owning the Room

– Cuddy, Amy. *Presence: Bringing Your Boldest Self to Your Biggest Challenges*. Little, Brown Spark, 2015.

– Ekman, Paul. *Emotions Revealed: Recognizing Faces and Feelings to Improve Communication and Emotional Life*. 2nd ed. Holt Paperbacks, 2007.

– Lao Tzu. *Tao Te Ching: A New English Version*. Translated by Stephen Mitchell. Harper & Row, 1988.

– The Bible. Gospel accounts.

– Tolle, Eckhart. *The Power of Now: A Guide to Spiritual Enlightenment*. New World Library, 1997.

Chapter 9: From Reaction to Response

– Bhagavad Gita. Translated and with commentary by Eknath Easwaran. Nilgiri Press, 2007.

– The Bible. Gospel References (e.g., John 8:6).

– Cuddy, Amy. *Presence: Bringing Your Boldest Self to Your Biggest Challenges.* Little, Brown Spark, 2015.

– Dass, Ram. *Be Here Now.* Lama Foundation, 1971.

– Edmondson, Amy C. *The Fearless Organization. Creating Psychological Safety in the Workplace for Learning, Innovation, and Growth.* Wiley, 2018.

– Ekman, Paul. *Emotions Revealed: Recognizing Faces and Feelings to Improve Communication and Emotional Life.* 2nd ed. Holt Paperbacks, 2007.

– Goleman, Daniel. *Emotional Intelligence: Why It Can Matter More Than IQ.* Bantam Books, 1995.

– Hall, Edward T. *Beyond Culture.* Anchor Books, 1976.

– Marsh, Jason. "Is Attention the Secret to Emotional Intelligence?" *Greater Good Magazine* (UC Berkeley), 2013.

– Selig, Paul. *I Am the Word: A Guide to the Consciousness of Man's Self in a Transitioning Time.* Jeremy P. Tarcher/ Penguin, 2010.

Chapter 10: Speak to Lead

– The Bible. Gospel references (e.g., John 1:1).

Chapter 11: Coaching as Culture

– McKinsey & Company. "The People Power of Transformation. 2017. https://www. mckinsey.com/~/ media/mckinsey/business%20functions/people%20 and%20organizational%20performance/our%20 insights/ the%20people%20power%20of%20transformations/ the-people-power-of-transformations.pdf.

– Roberts, Jane. *The Seth Material.* Prentice-Hall, 1970.

– Stanier, Michael Bungay. *The Coaching Habit: Say Less, Ask More, and Change the Way You Lead Forever.* Page Two Publishing, 2016.

– Thich Nhat Hanh. *The Art of Communicating: Mastering Life's Most Important Skill Through Mindfulness, Personal Growth, and Effective Interpersonal Relations.* HarperOne, 2013.

Chapter 12: The Mind Flip

– Anka, Darryl and Luana Ewing. *Bashar: Blueprint for Change, A Message From Our Future.* New Solutions Publishing, 1990.

– Johnson, Barry. *Polarity Management: Identifying and Managing Unsolvable Problems.* Human Resource Development Press, 1992.

– Laloux, Frederic. *Reinventing Organizations: A Guide to Creating Organizations Inspired by the Next Stage of Human Consciousness.* Nelson Parker, 2014.

– Lencioni, Patrick. *The Five Dysfunctions of a Team: A Leadership Fable.* Jossey-Bass, 2002.

– Wilber, Ken. *A Theory of Everything: An Integral Vision for Business, Politics, Science, and Spirituality.* Shambhala, 2000.

Chapter 13: Crossing the Threshold

– Dass, Ram. *Still Here: Embracing Aging, Changing, and Dying.* Riverhead Books, 2000.

– Goleman, Daniel. *Emotional Intelligence: Why It Can Matter More Than IQ.* Bantam Books, 1995.

– Hatfield, Elaine, John T. Cacioppo, and Richard L. Rapson. *Emotional Contagion.* Cambridge University Press, 1994.

– Petriglieri, Gianpiero. "The Psychology Behind Effective Crisis Leadership." *Harvard Business Review*, 2020.

– Rodenburg, *The Second Circle: How to Use Positive Energy for Success in Every Situation*. W. W. Norton & Company, 2008.

– Rumi. *Teachings of Rumi*. Edited by Andrew Harvey. Shambhala, 1999.

– Rumi. *The Essential Rumi*. Translated by Coleman Barks and John Moyne. HarperSan Francisco, 2004.

Chapter 14: Emotional Tone as Leadership

– The Bible. Gospel references (e.g., Luke 5:16).

– Brach, Tara. *Radical Acceptance: Embracing Your Life with the Heart of a Buddha*. Bantam Books, 2003.

– Covey, Stephen M. R. *The Speed of Trust: The One Thing That Changes Everything*. Free Press, 2006.

– Dutton, Jane E. *Energize Your Workplace: How to Create and Sustain High-Quality Connections at Work*. Jossey-Bass, 2003.

– Ekman, Paul. *Emotions Revealed: Recognizing Faces and Feelings to Improve Communication and Emotional Life*. 2nd ed., Holt Paperbacks, 2007.

– Hatfield, Elaine, John T. Cacioppo, and Richard L. Rapson. 1993. *Emotional Contagion (Studies in Emotion and Social Interaction)*. Cambridge University Press, 1994.

– Rumi. *The Essential Rumi*. Translated by Coleman Barks and John Moyne. HarperSanFrancisco, 2004.

Chapter 15: When the Climb Stalls

– Amabile, Teresa M., and Steven J. Kramer. "The Crisis of Identity in Retirement." *Harvard Business Review*, 2019.

– Bridges, William and Susan Bridges. 2004. *Transitions: Making Sense of Life's Changes*. De Capo Press, 2004.

– Cahill, Kevin E., Michael D. Giandrea, and Joseph F. Quinn. "Retirement Patterns and the Macroeconomy, 1992–2010: The Prevalence and Determinants of Bridge Jobs, Phased Retirement, and Reentry Among Three Recent Cohorts of Older Americans." *The Gerontologist*, 55(3): 384–403, 2015.

– Covey, Stephen R. *The 7 Habits of Highly Effective People*. Simon & Schuster, 1989.

– Harris, Lee. *Energy Speaks: Messages from Spirit on Living, Loving, and Awakening*. New World Library, 2019.

– Hicks, Esther and Jerry Hicks. *Ask and It Is Given: Learning to Manifest Your Desires*. Hay House, 2004.

– Kim, Jungmeen E. and Phyllis Moen. "Retirement Transitions, Gender, and Psychological Well-Being: A Life-Course, Ecological Model." *The Journals of Gerontology: Series B*, 57(3): P212–P222, 2002.

– Selig, Paul. *The Book of Knowing and Worth: A Channeled Text*. Jeremy P. Tarcher/Penguin, 2013.

– Wang, Mo and Xiaodan Dong. "Retirement and Cardiovascular Disease: A 15-Year Longitudinal Analysis." *Journal of Epidemiology & Community Health*, 73(7): 633–640, 2019.

– Whitmore, John. *Coaching for Performance: The Principles and Practice of Coaching and Leadership*. John Murray Business, 1992.

Chapter 16: The Long View

– Frei, Frances X. and Anne Morriss. "Begin With Trust: The First Step to Becoming a Genuinely Empowering Leader." *Harvard Business Review*, May-June, 2020.

– Kimmerer, Robin Wall. 2015. *Braiding Sweetgrass: Indigenous Wisdom, Scientific Knowledge, and the Teachings of Plants.* Milkweed Editions, 2013.

– Zak, Paul J. "The Neuroscience of Trust." *Harvard Business Review*, January 2017.

Chapter 17: Integration

– The Bible. Gospel teachings.

– Dass, Ram. *Be Here Now.* Lama Foundation, 1971.

– Dass, Ram and Mirabai Bush. *Walking Each Other Home: Conversations on Loving and Dying.* Sounds True, 2018.

INDEX

ABOUT THE AUTHOR

Kathryn Lowell is an executive coach and image consultant who has spent more than two decades helping leaders uncover blind spots and accelerate their success. A Yale graduate with an MBA from UCLA, she began her career on Wall Street before becoming the first Westerner to work in finance in post-communist Hungary.

In 2001, she turned her focus to leadership development, fascinated by a single question: Why do some leaders rise while others with equal talent and credentials stall? That inquiry led her to blend image consulting with executive coaching into a distinctive practice that has shaped countless leaders through coaching, workshops, and speaking engagements.

She is known for helping leaders at pivotal career moments step into authentic, visible presence. A self-professed workaholic, Kathryn's favorite way to recharge is traveling with her husband, Michael Spivey, for cultural immersion—a practice that keeps her grounded in wonder and curiosity.

Kathryn welcomes your questions and requests at
kathrynlowell@tuta.com

Visit her website, www.modernleadersjourney.com,
to learn how to order this book and find more information
about the services she offers.

www.ingramcontent.com/pod-product-compliance
Lightning Source LLC
Chambersburg PA
CBHW021213130626
46554CB00004B/1205